A Touch of Spice

With Greek and American Flair

Kali Orexi

(Good Appetite)

We Share My Mom's Favorite Treasures

Written by

Stella Apostolos
and son
Spencer H. Apostolos

authorHOUSE®

AuthorHouse™
1663 Liberty Drive
Bloomington, IN 47403
www.authorhouse.com
Phone: 1-800-839-8640

First published by AuthorHouse 10/15/2009

ISBN: 978-1-4490-3031-5 (e)
ISBN: 978-1-4490-3030-8 (sc)

Library of Congress Control Number: 2009910490

Printed in the United States of America
Bloomington, Indiana

This book is printed on acid-free paper.

Dedication

I found myself faced with bags full of countless recipes after losing both my parents last year.
These recipes are written on scrap paper, food stained paper, envelopes, pieces of cardboard and anything my Mom had handy to write on at the moment, along with famous quotations she loved.

I didn't know what to do with this lifetime of memories!

When we visited my Mom and Dad we could almost always count on them being in the kitchen, or in their beautiful garden.

I can see my Mom at the stove and Dad rolling out the dough for a peta or beating the eggs or cleaning up. "A man's job" he would say.
He loved washing the dishes.

You never left their home with an empty stomach.
That was part of who they were.

My Mom was my very best friend--my soul mate.
My Dad was my inspiration throughout my entire life.

I loved them dearly and miss them every day.

After looking at these bags for over a year my son Spencer and I decided to share their favorite recipes.
We hope you enjoy them as much as we did putting them together.

In memory of my parents-- We dedicate this cookbook to

James and Helen Manekas

A Morning Prayer

Let me today do something that will take
  A little sadness from the world's vast store,
And may I be so favored as to make
  Of joy's too scanty sum a little more.

Let me not hurt, by any selfish deed
  Or thoughtless word, the heart of foe or friend.
Nor would I pass unseeing worthy need,
  Or sin by silence when I should defend.

However meager be my worldly wealth,
  Let me give something that shall aid my kind-
A word of courage, or a thought of health
  Dropped as I pass for troubled hearts to find.

Let me tonight look back across the span
  "Twixt dawn and dark, and to my conscience say-
Because of some good act to beast or man-
  "The world is better that I lived today."

Ella Wheeler Wilcox

Appetizers

Appetizers

Stuffed Mushrooms
Spinach Squares
Crabmeat with Mushrooms
Party Fruit Platter
Cheese Squares
Spinach Quiche
Sausage and Cheese Balls
Potato Cheese Balls
Oyster Puffs
Shrimp Spread
Cream Cheese Balls
Cheese Balls
Clam Dip
Hawaiian Balls
California Taco Dip
Red Wine Spread
Cocktail Hot Dogs
Pistachio Cheese Spread
Cheese Tortillas
Cheese Squares
Party Cream Cheesy Sandwiches
Asparagus Roll Ups
Mushroom Turnovers
Olive Cheese Puffs
Shrimp Cocktail Hot Sauce
Quick Ham Rolls
Sugared Pecans

Basic Helpful Cooking Terms

Al dente---Cook until tender but still firm to the bite.

Au gratin---Food cooked in sauce- covered with cheese or crumbs and browned.

Bake blind---To bake a pastry case without the filling. Fill the bottom of the pastry dish with dried beans while cooking.

Bind----To thicken a liquid by adding flour.

Blanch------Put food into boiling water for just a few seconds, or minutes, then into cold water and drain.

Bouillon----Meat broth

Bouquet garni ----A mixture of herbs tied in a bundle-added to soups and stews for flavor.

Carve---Slice meats into pieces.

Clarify----Remove bits and pieces from liquid by heating-then straining the liquid.

Cream---Beat until soft and creamy.

Croutons----Small-bite size bread cubes-browned till crispy.

Drizzle---Pour liquid very slowly.

Emulsify---Combine 2 liquids that wouldn't ordinarily mix.-
-- e.g. oil and vinegar

Fillet---Remove skin and bones from raw meat.

Fry----Cook in oil or fat product.

Garnish--Decorate your dish.

Glaze---Use a beaten egg, egg white or sugar to coat food -to give it a shiny appearance.

Knead---Work the dough with your hands-pressing the dough , folding towards you and press with the palms of your hands. Repeat-following the recipe directions.

Bake--To cook in the oven at temperatures according to directions.

Fold--Gently bringing spoon or spatula down in the center of the mixture, across the bottom and back up to the top. Repeat until well incorporated.

Sauté---Cook quickly in small amount of oil or butter over direct heat.

Scald--- To heat a liquid , usually refers to milk-to just below the boiling point.

Dice---Cut into small pieces--¼ inch or less.

Pare---To peel off outer skin--like potatoes, apples or cukes.

Moist heat---Gentle simmer-not boiling.

Grate---Cutting ingredients using a grater to cut into tiny pieces.

Shred---To cut into very thin strips.

Dredge---Before cooking-cover food with flour or bread crumbs.

Whip---Beat with a mixer or whisk vigorously.

Julienne---Cut into thin -long strips.

Beat---Mix vigorously with a fork, whisk, or mixer

Dutch oven---A pan for deep cooking with a tight fitting cover.

Caramelize---To cook over low heat to develop a golden brown color.

Poach---Cook in simmering liquid such as eggs or fish.

Steep---Soak food in hot liquid to absorb the flavor.

Simmer---Cook food in liquid almost to the boiling point-but not bubbling.

Blend---Mix completely until smooth.

Sear---Cook over high heat to brown quickly. Then reduce heat to complete cooking.

Papillote--- Cook food in foil or baking paper.

Pare---Peel veggies or fruit.

Parboil---Boil until partially cooked.

Pickle---To preserve in brine or oil and vinegar.

Puree--Mashed or blended to a smooth, thick consistency

Reduce---Decrease the volume by boiling to a thickened stage.

Skim---After boiling- remove scum from top of pot.

Zest---Grate outer layer of skin from fruit without the inner layer of pith.

Marinate---Allow food to soak and tenderize in a prepared liquid.

Puree---To grind, mash or blend food until it becomes thick and smooth.

Beat---To mix completely and vigorously with a fork, blender or beater.

Baste--- To put liquids, drippings, marinade or butter over food during the cooking process.

Cut in---Usually used for pie crusts, mixing butter or shortening into dry mixture by cutting it in with a knife or pastry cutter.

Roll out---Usually refers to dough. To flatten or spread out with a rolling pin.

Mix---Combine ingredients evenly with a spoon or mixer.

Sift---Put dry ingredients through a fine mesh or strainer to remove lumps.

***** FYI-----

TOO MUCH SALT ???

***Adding a raw potato to broth or soup and simmer until potato is cooked will absorb some of the salt. --

Measure Equivalents

1 tablespoon-----3 teaspoons
1 cup-----   16 tbsp.
1 cup-----   48 tsp.
½ cup----   8 tbsp.
2/3 cup---   10 tbsp. + 2 tsp.
¾ cup---   12 tbsp.
1/3 cup---   5 tbsp. +1 Tsp.
¼ cup---   4 tbsp.
1/6 cup---   2 tbsp. + 2 tsp.
1/8 cup---   2 tbsp.
1/16 cup---   1 tbsp.
8 fluid oz.--   1 cup
1 pint---   2 cups
4 cups----   1 quart
3/8 cup--   6 tbsp.
1 gallon--   4 quarts
16 oz.---   1 pound

Stuffed Mushrooms

Lg. button mushrooms--3-4 per person
    (Remove stems, chop and set aside)
1 medium onion-finely diced
5 strips bacon-cooked crispy
1 lg. box chicken stuffing
3 slices American cheese
1 tbsp. olive oil
1 tbsp. butter
Salt and pepper

Set mushrooms onto baking sheet, caps down--set aside.
In a non stick frying pan sauté onions and mushrooms stems in olive oil and butter until golden. Add crumbled bacon and mix well. Add salt and pepper to taste--
Set aside.

Make stuffing according to box directions then add 1 tsp. olive oil,1 tbsp. butter and 3 tbsp. water.
Salt and pepper mushroom caps and drizzle olive oil into each cap.
Add a small piece of American cheese into each cap.
Mix onion ,bacon and mushroom stems and fold into stuffing mix.

Fill caps with mixture. Pile high! Sprinkle olive oil over each one.
Bake at 375 deg. Till soft-not mushy.-about 25-30 min.
Stuffing will be crispy

Spinach Squares

4 tbsp. margarine
3 eggs
1 cup flour
1 cup milk
1 tbsp. baking powder
8 oz. grated cheddar cheese
8 oz. grated mozzarella cheese
1 tsp grated onion
2 pkgs. Frozen spinach- thawed and drained

Melt margarine in pan. Beat eggs in a bowl and add flour, milk and baking powder.
Add spinach, onion, and cheese . Mix well.
Pour into oblong pan. Sprinkle with grated cheese Bake at 350 deg. For 35-45 min.

Crabmeat with Mushrooms

Approx. 24-25 medium mushrooms
1-1/2 cups flaked crabmeat
2 eggs
3 tbs. mayonnaise
¼ cup minced green onion
½ cup soft bread crumbs
2 tsp. lemon juice
1/3 cup melted butter

Dip washed mushroom caps into melted butter. Place them cap side down into buttered baking dish.
Combine crab meat eggs, mayonnaise, green onion, lemon juice chopped mushroom stems, and half the bread crumbs. Fill mushrooms with mixture, sprinkle with remaining bread crumbs and dot with 2 tbs. butter. Bake in mod. Oven, 375 deg. For 15 minutes.

Party Fruit Platter

1 cup plain yogurt	1 lg banana-sliced
½ cup maple syrup	2 cups strawberries-halved
2 tbsp. lemon juice	2 cups pineapple chunks-drained
¼ tsp. cinnamon	2 kiwi- sliced
2 pears-sliced	2 apples sliced

Dip bananas, apples and pears in lemon juice to prevent discoloration.

To make dressing---

Combine yogurt, syrup,1 tsp. lemon juice, cinnamon and mix well.
Arrange fruit around a platter with the dressing in a bowl in the center.

Cheese Squares

Make one day ahead---

1 loaf good quality bread
1 lb. grated cheese
3 sticks butter or margarine
2 eggs
½ tsp garlic salt --   ½ tsp. onion salt
½ tsp. Worcestershire sauce

Mix cheese with butter, add eggs, one at a time, then seasonings. Beat well with mixer. (can be done by hand) Remove crust from bread. Spread softened mixture all over bread - top, bottom and sides. Place on lightly greased cookie sheet. Refrigerate over night.
Can be frozen now or bake at 375 deg. For 15-20 minutes until bubbly.

Spinach Quiche

½ cup spinach (frozen) needs to be thawed and drained
3 eggs
½ lb. feta cheese
Cream - ½ and ½
Crisco or vegetable shortening

Put eggs, cheese and spinach in a measuring cup . Add cream to make 2 cups.

Crust--

1-¼ c. flour
1-¼ c. margarine -----   All ingredients must be chilled.
2 tbsp. Crisco   Ready made pie crust can be used
½ c. water-chilled

Cube margarine and add Crisco. Blend in mixer with flour. Add chilled water and mix to make a dough.

Remove and form dough into a ball and chill overnight if you can or at least 2 hours.
Roll out dough onto a pie tin pressing into corners. Cut off excess.

Pre heat oven at 350 deg. Prick dough with a fork. Place any dried beans over dough to keep crust from bubbling. Bake until brown.

Pour spinach mixture onto crust. Sprinkle top with feta cheese and add pieces of butter.
Bake at 375deg. 30-40 minutes. Allow to stand 5 minutes before swerving.

Sausage and Cheese Balls

3 cups instant biscuit mix
1 lb. sausage-remove from casings
1 lb. sharp grated cheddar cheese
1 onion-chopped and sautéed in butter

Incorporate cheese with crumble sausage and add biscuit mix.
Form into small balls and bake on cookie sheet at 400 deg. For 15 minutes.

Can be frozen before baking, and used as needed. Makes about 60.

Potato Cheese Balls

8 medium potatoes
1 cup grated cheddar cheese
3 tbsp. parmesan cheese
Salt and pepper
Milk
3 tbsp. butter
2 egg yolks
Bread crumbs

Mash the potatoes. Add salt and pepper and small amount of milk.
(potatoes should be on the stiff side .)
Add cheeses, butter and egg yolks. Blend well.
Form into tennis size balls or smaller.
First dip them in the bread crumbs, then dip them in the beaten egg then
again in the bread crumbs with a few shakes of the parmesan cheese.

Bake at 400deg. For 20-30 minutes.-- These can be made ahead and
refrigerated . Place on wax paper and cover with wax paper. Bring to room
temp. before baking, ½ to ¾ hour.

Oyster Puffs

4 slices of white bread-toasted
2 tbsp. soft butter
¾ tsp. mustard
8 oz. can oysters, drained
¼ cup grated Velveeta cheese

Cut crusts off bread. Cut bread into four squares. Mix butter and mustard, spread on toast. Put an oyster on each piece and top with cheese. Broil for 5 minutes or until browned and hot .

Serve immediately

Shrimp Spread

½ lb. cooked, cleaned shrimp
½ cup butter
2 tsp. pale dry sherry
1 tsp. lemon juice
1 small onion-finely chopped
1 tsp. grated lemon
¼ tsp. mace
¼ tsp. dry mustard
½ tsp. cayenne

Finely grind the shrimp. Cream the butter and blend with sherry, lemon juice onion, and seasonings. Add shrimp and blend. Place in oiled 2 cup mold and chill. Dip the base of the mold in warm water to unmold when ready to serve.

Serve with crackers or cocktail brown bread

Cream Cheese Balls

1-8oz. Pkg. cream cheese- softened
¾ cup sharp cheddar cheese
Grated chopped nuts
¼ cup sour cream

Blend cheeses and sour cream until smooth.
Chill for 1 hour then roll into ½ inch balls.
Roll in nuts and heap them in the center of a serving dish.
Place assorted crackers around them

Cheese Balls

1 stick butter or margarine
1 cup grated cheese
1 cup unsifted flower
1/8 tsp red pepper
¼ tsp. salt

Mix all ingredients in a lg. bowl and roll into small balls. Place on ungreased cookie sheet in a 200 deg. oven for 1 hour.

Clam Dip

2-8 oz. pkgs. Cream cheese
Dash of seasoned salt
2 tsp. Worcestershire sauce
1 can minced clams

Soften cream cheese, add salt, clams with liquid -slowly (1 tbs. at a time)
Add Worcestershire sauce. Mix with a beater until it is the consistency of
heavy cream.

Serve in a shell--   6-8 servings

Hawaiian Balls

*make a day ahead *

2 pkgs. 8 oz. cream cheese- softened
2 cups chopped pecans
1 small can crushed pineapples-drained
¼ cup finely chopped green peppers
2 tsp. finely chopped onions
2 tbs. seasoned salt

Combine everything except 1 cup of the pecans.
Chill mixture for one day.
Shape into balls and roll them over the remaining pecans

California Taco Dip

1-16 0z. Can refried beans
1 envelope Taco Seasoning Mix
Grated cheddar cheese
1 small can whole chilies -chopped
Chopped tomatoes
½ pint sour cream
Chopped scallions (green onions)

Mix refried beans with taco mix. Spread mixture on serving platter.
Spread chilies over beans (remove seeds and pits if you don't like it too
Hot.)
Top with a layer of grated cheese. Then a layer of tomatoes.
Spread sour cream over tomatoes and sprinkle chopped scallions on top.

   Refrigerate until served--

Red Wine Spread

3 0z. Roquefort cheese
3 tbs. Sherry or red wine (one that you would drink)
3 tbsp. butter

Blend well with wooden spoon.
Keep refrigerated until needed.
Serve with crackers

Cocktail Hot Dogs

1 or 2 pkgs. of cocktail hotdogs (or use regular size and cut in smaller pieces)
1 bottle Current jelly
Mustard to taste

Melt jelly (stove or microwave). Add mustard.
Simmer for 30 seconds.
Pour over cooked hot dogs.
Serve with toothpicks

Pistachio-cheese spread

1-3 oz. pkg. Roquefort cheese
1- 3 0z. Pkg. cream cheese
1 tbs. heavy cream
1 tsp. minced onion
2 tbsp. chopped ripe olives
½ cup blanched, chopped pistachio nuts

Combine all above ingredients and chill
Serve on crackers or as a veggie or bread stick dip.

Cheese Tortillas

4 tortillas
Chopped green pepper
Butter or margarine
1 chopped onion
grated cheddar cheese

Spread 4 tortillas with butter or margarine and add grated cheddar cheese on top. Add chopped green peppers and chopped onion.

  Bake at350 deg. Until cheese is melted. Cut into 4 to 8 pieces as you would a pie and serve hot taco sauce .

Cheese Squares

2 cups Bisquick
1 cup milk (whole or skim)
2 eggs or (1 small carton egg beaters)
½ cup chopped parsley
½ lb. feta cheese- crumbled
¼ cup margarine

Preheat oven to 350 deg. Melt margarine. Use a small amt. to grease bottom of 7x11 pan.

Combine milk, eggs, parsley and cheese. Stir in Bisquick. Stir in melted margarine. Pour into greased pan.
Bake For 20-25 min. Cut into squares. Serve hot or at room temp.

Party cream cheesy sandwiches

2-3oz. Pkgs. Softened cream cheese
¼ cup deviled ham (one 2-¼ oz.can)
8 slices bacon -cooked crisp and diced
½ cup sliced pimento stuffed olives
36 slices of party rye bread

Mix together cream cheese, deviled ham, bacon and olives. Spread bread
with butter or margarine. Spread 18 slices of bread with cheese mixture and
cover with remaining 18 bread slices.

* sandwiches can be frozen *

Asparagus Roll Ups

12 slices of bread (good thick consistency) cut off crusts
12 slices bacon-cooked and crumbled
2-8 oz. pkgs cream cheese- softened
12 cooked asparagus spears
Melted butter or margarine
Tabasco sauce

Roll bread to flatten. Blend bacon with cheese and a few drops of Tabasco sauce. Spread mixture on bread, cut in half. Lay asparagus on bread. Roll up and pinch together seam side down and brush with butter .Put under broiler 2nd level until slightly brown and hot.

* Watch carefully *

Mushroom Turnovers

1 stick margarine (room temp.)
1 lg. pkg. cream cheese (softened)
1 cup flour

Mix ingredients well. Roll dough out on floured wax paper.
Cut into rounds with biscuit cutter.

Filling:
Combine:
½ lb. mushrooms- minced.
1 onion -minced
1 tsp. salt
¼ tsp. thyme
¼ cup sour cream

Stuff dough and fold in half Use a fork top seal the edges.
Bake at 450 deg. For 12-15 minutes

Serve hot

Olive Cheese Puffs

2 cups grated cheddar cheese
½ tsp. paprika
1 cup all purpose flour
Chopped olives
1-2 tsp. water

Combine all ingredients well.
Add 1-2 tsp. water, more if necessary and mix well.
Shape mixture into small balls and roll them in the olives.
Bake at 400 deg. For 15-20 minutes.

(Freezes well)

Shrimp Cocktail Hot Sauce

1-14 oz. bottle of catsup
4 shakes of Tabasco sauce
3 tsp. horse radish
Juice of 1 lemon

Combine all ingredients and chill

Quick Ham Rolls

Sliced ham (your choice)
Roquefort or Blue Cheese dressing
Parsley flakes
Paprika

Spread ham slices with cheese spread. Roll up jelly roll fashion. Slice in ½ inch pieces. Dip into parsley flakes and sprinkle with paprika.

Sugared Pecans

1 cup sugar
¼ cup evaporated milk
2 tbs. water
¼ tsp. cinnamon
¼ tsp. vanilla

Combine all ingredients in a saucepan and cook until soft ball temperature is reached. Stir in 2 cups of nuts. Turn out on wax paper on a cookie sheet to cool.

******   Helen's Helpful Hints   ******

(Organic Pesticides)

1 cup vegetable oil
1 tbsp. dish detergent   Mix together well !!

Use 1 pint water   Mix together and
2 tsp. oil   Spray every 10 days

Safe for flowers and vegetables   (except cabbage)

****Really Works well ****

Soups

SOUPS

Kremidosoúpa------Onion Soup
Revithosoúpa-------Chickpea Soup
Youvarlákia Avgolemono---Greek Meatball-Egg Lemon Soup
Tomato Soúpa-------Tomato Soup
Sausage Pasta Soup
Hamburg Florentine and Onion Soup
Creamy Broccoli Soup
Tomato Orzo Soup
Family Style Beef Stew
Hearty Cheddar Cheese Soup
Oyster Stew
French Onion Soup
Leek Soup
Chicken Chili
Mom's Hot Dog Soup
Lentil Soup
Cabbage and Hamburg Soup
Avgolémono-------Greek Egg Lemon Soup
Junk Soup---Family Style
Corn Chowder
Chili
Tomato Rice Soup with Feta
Fassolátha----------Bean Soup with Hot Peppers

Great Garnishes For Soups---For More Flavor and Appeal

Lemon slices
Chopped parsley
Sour cream or Crème Fraiche
Croutons or toasted bread
Bacon bits
Chives
Dumplings
Scallions
Oyster crackers
Shredded cheeses
Hot rice in center of bowl
Brown bread
Paper thin mushrooms
Hard boiled eggs-sliced thin
Shaved carrots
Chinese noodles
Fried tortilla strips
Pasta noodles
Roasted garlic
Alpha sprouts
Thin peels of grated, colorful veggies
Melon slices
Feta cheese
Dollop of butternut squash
Dollop of yogurt or sour cream
Diced ham or chicken
Tiny meatballs
Sliced sausages
Soy sauce
Balsamic vinegar
Spiced oils
Toasted nuts

***You may use carefully prepared fish products
such as scallops, shrimp and clams

Kremidosoúpa----------Onion Soup

4- lg. onions-chopped
1 cup olive oil
salt and pepper
1 tsp. corn flour
parmesan cheese

Using a saucepan saute onions in oil. Add 6 cups of boiling water.
Add salt and pepper to taste and cook on low heat for about 15 minutes.

Mix corn flour with a little water and pour mixture into saucepan.
Simmer on low heat for about 5 more minutes-stirring frequently.

****Sprinkle parmesan cheese over each individual bowl.
           or
****Garnish with bacon bits, and/or chopped parsley--so good!

Revithosoúpa-----Chickpea Soup

1 cup dried chickpeas
6-8 cups water
¼ cup oil
½ tsp. baking powder
1 lg. onion-chopped
2-3 lemons -to taste
1 small celery stalk- finely cut
1 small carrot- small dice
salt and pepper
1 tbsp. flour

Soak the chickpeas in a lg. pot of water the night before cooking.
Rinse and drain the next day. Place chickpeas in a bowl with the baking
powder for about 1 hour. Coat them well.

Remove as much of the skin as possible by rubbing the peas between the
palms of your hands. -Rinse and drain.

*****To make the soup***

Place chickpeas in a pot of water and bring to a boil.
Skim off any foam that forms on top of the soup while cooking.

Reduce heat and add carrots and onions and simmer for about 2 hours to
make sure chickpeas are tender. Stir occasionally . Add more water if
needed.
Season with salt and pepper, if necessary, and add oil.

In a small bowl mix the lemon juice with the flour until well blended.

Add one or two cups of the liquid from the soup pot - to the lemon and
flour mixture. Mix well!

Then add mixture back into pot and stir.

Youvarlákia Avgolémono ---Greek Meatball-Egg Lemon Soup

1-½ lbs. ground beef
1 lg. onion-finely diced
2-14.5 cans chicken broth (or stock)
1 lg. can tomato sauce
1-¼ cups lemon juice-or less-to taste
7 eggs
¾ cups long grain rice-uncooked
salt and pepper
¼ tsp. garlic powder
1 tsp. dried oregano
¼ cup ketchup

In a lg. pot add chicken broth, tomato sauce, salt and pepper.
Fill pot with water to make 6 qts. Bring to a simmer.

In a lg. bowl- combine meat, onions, salt, pepper, oregano, ketchup, garlic
powder, rice and 1 egg slightly beaten.
Mix until all ingredients are well incorporated. (hands are the best tools)

Shape into small meatballs and add to simmering soup pot . Cook for about
20 minutes till rice is tender.

--------To prepare Avgolémono---Egg Lemon Mixture----

In a lg. bowl beat 6 eggs for 3 minutes till eggs are frothy. While beating
constantly, drizzle in the lemon juice--very slowly.
Then add about 2 cups of the hot broth, from the soup pot ,to the eggs
again- very slowly, beating constantly.

Then add egg mixture back into soup pot. Stir carefully not to break the
meatballs.

*****Serve with Greek bread and salad
                    *** you can cut recipe in half

Tomáto Soúpa---------Tomato Soup

1 stalk celery- chopped
¾ cup olive oil
1 carrot-cut in small thin pieces
parsley-chopped
1-¼ cup -tiny pasta (for soups) --your choice
1 onion- sliced thin
1 lb. tomatoes-sliced very small (can use canned)

Cook pasta as directed, drain and set aside.

Add about 3 pints water into a saucepan. Add tomatoes, carrots, celery and onion. Bring to a boil-then cook over medium heat for about 30 minutes.

Mash the tomatoes in the saucepan that have been cooking. Add salt and pepper and parsley.   Mix well.
Add cooked pasta and simmer for about 5 minutes.

Sausage Pasta Soup

1 lb. sweet sausage
1 lg can crushed tomatoes
1 lg. can diced tomatoes- with liquid
2-14 oz. cans chicken broth
salt and pepper
1 tsp. oregano
1-8oz. Can tomato sauce
1 small onion- chopped
1 tbsp. Italian seasoning
1 pkg. frozen assorted veggies
½ lb. short pasta-- (your choice) cooked and drained

Add about 3 inches of water in a lg. soup pot. Add whole sausages
And bring to a boil. Simmer for about 20 minutes. Turn them occasionally.

Remove sausages from pan-cut into pieces and place back in pot.
Add crushed tomatoes, diced tomatoes, onion, salt and pepper, tomato
sauce , chicken broth oregano and Italian seasoning. Stir well.

Cook for 1 hour, or longer, on low heat.
Mix well during cooking.

Add cooked pasta and veggies, Cook till all is tender. Re-season if
necessary.

****** Great idea!!

Hamburg Florentine and Onion Soup

1 lb. ground Hamburg
5 cups water
2 cans chicken broth
2 cups -peeled, cubed potatoes
2 cups cabbage-chopped
1 cup onions-chopped
salt and pepper
1 bay leaf
1-28 oz. can diced tomatoes -with liquid
1-14.5 oz. can green beans and liquid
1-9oz. pkg. frozen spinach-chopped
1.2 tsp. garlic powder
1/3 cup barley-uncooked

Use a 5 qt. saucepot--

Sauté ground beef and drain .Stir in all the ingredients except the spinach.
Bring to a boil and reduce heat.
Cover, simmer for 30 minutes.

Add spinach and cover. Continue simmering about 20 minutes longer. Stir occasionally.
Remove bay leaf and allow to sit for about 10 minutes before serving .

****Serve with brown bread!!

Creamy Broccoli Soup

1 lg. bag frozen broccoli
1 can chicken broth
1 cup light cream
1 pkg. 8 oz. shredded Swiss cheese
Cornstarch -dissolved in water to thicken

Cook broccoli in chicken broth till tender. Mash the broccoli -by hand or in blender. Add cream, then cornstarch to the right thickening consistency.

Add cheese slowly, stirring until completely melted and smooth.

***Adjust liquids if too thick…

Tomato Orzo Soup

1 medium onion-finely chopped
1 carrot-cut into thin strips then finely chopped
3 tbsp. oil
1 lg. can diced tomatoes-with liquid
1 lg. can tomato sauce   1-¼ cups orzo
2 cans chicken broth   salt and pepper
water   1 tsp. garlic powder
1 tbsp. margarine or butter   ½ lemon -(more to taste)

In lg. soup pan---

Sauté onion and carrots in oil and 1 cup water till tender. (add more water if
necessary while cooking) Mix well.
Add salt, pepper, and garlic powder. Pour in chicken broth and 4-½ cups
water. Bring to a boil.

Add orzo bring back up to a boil and lower heat. Cook till tender (not
mushy) About 15-20 minutes-stirring often.

Add diced tomatoes , tomato sauce and butter. Cook another 2 minutes
On low heat.
Remove from heat- squeeze lemon into pot. Pour into bowls and sprinkle
tops with parmesan cheese.

****If soup thickens too much add more water and/or chicken broth.
****Serve with garlic bread and salad--great for lunch or
Dinner!!

Family Style Beef Stew

2 cans chicken broth
2-½ lbs. chuck beef-cut into 1-½ inch cubes
1 lg. onion- chopped
4-5 stalks celery- cut in bite size pieces
6 lg. carrots-peeled and sliced in rounds
salt and pepper
1 tbsp. oregano
¼ cup Worcestershire sauce
1 lg. can mushrooms
6 lg. potatoes- peeled and cubed
1 lg. can tomato sauce
½ cup olive oil
1 lg. can diced tomatoes -with liquid
½ tsp. garlic powder
1 small can sweet peas

Marinate beef in Worcestershire sauce for ½ hour.
Sauté onion in oil till tender and add to beef and Worcestershire sauce.
Cook for about 20 minutes. Add 2 cans chicken broth , salt, pepper, garlic
powder, and oregano. Mix well.

Simmer till meat is tender.
Add carrots, celery and mushrooms and enough water to cover veggies.
Cook on medium heat till all ingredients are tender.
Add potatoes -cook till fork tender.

Add in the tomato sauce and diced tomatoes. (with liquid)
Simmer on low heat another 10 minutes.
Re-season if necessary.

*** Serve with Italian bread--Serves 6-8

****Recipe can be cut in half

Hearty Cheddar Cheese Soup

2 tsp. margarine
1 tsp. vegetable oil
½ cup onion-chopped
2 tsp. flour
½ tsp. dry mustard
1-½ cups chicken broth
1 cup milk
¾ cup shredded cheddar cheese
½ cup celery- chopped

Sauté onion and celery in the margarine and oil for about 5 minutes till veggies are tender. (do not brown)
Blend in the flour and mustard and continue stirring for about 2 minutes.
Add the chicken broth and simmer about 3-4 minutes- stirring occasionally.

Add milk, bring to a simmer and stir in the cheese.

****Serve with more cheese if necessary!

Oyster Stew

1-8 oz. can oysters with liquid
1 cup ½ and ½
1 tbsp. butter
1 tbsp. Worcester sauce
pinch of paprika

Heat oysters with liquid and ½ and ½ over medium heat until it comes to a boil. Add butter and simmer 2-3 minutes .
Add paprika and Worcestershire sauce. Mix well.

***Garnish with scallions

*****Serve with oyster crackers

French Onion Soup

4 lg. onions -sliced thin
3 tbsp. margarine -or butter
4 cups beef broth- (canned or homemade)
1 tbsp. Worcestershire sauce
Parmesan cheese- grated
crusty rolls-sliced and toasted (or put under broiler)
Mozzarella cheese
Salt and pepper

Sauté onions in butter till caramelized and brown. Add beef broth
And Worcestershire sauce. Mix well. Season with salt and pepper.
Cook for about 15-20 minutes.

Pour soup into individual bowls. Put toast on top of soup bowl and sprinkle
generously with parmesan cheese . Add a small amount of mozzarella
cheese over top. Place bowl under broiler for a few seconds, enough to melt
the cheese.

*** Serves 4-6

Leek Soup

1 bunch leeks
1 lg. onion-chopped
3 lg. potatoes peeled and cubed
1 garlic clove- minced
salt and pepper to taste
1 tbsp. butter
1 tbsp. olive oil
4 cups chicken broth
½ cup heavy cream
2 tbsp. parsley- chopped

Wash leeks thoroughly- to remove all the sand.
Simmer the leeks, onions and garlic in butter and oil till tender.

Add broth and potatoes and cook on simmer for about 30 minutes.
Puree in blender -add cream, salt and pepper.

***Serve hot with sour cream or yogurt as a garnish to each bowl.

Chicken Chili

2 lg. chicken breasts--cook with skins on
  (then remove skin --cut into bite size piece.)
¼ cup basil-chopped
1 pkg. chili mix
1 lg. onion chopped
2 green peppers- diced
2 yellow peppers- diced
1 tbsp. crushed garlic--more to taste
2 lg. cans tomatoes chopped
salt and pepper
1 tsp. cumin
1 tsp. cocoa powder
1 tsp. garlic salt
cheese- for topping.
sour cream- for garnish

Sauté onions, garlic, and peppers till tender. Then add chili mix, salt and pepper, cumin, garlic salt, and tomatoes-mix well.

Add basil and cook for 30 minutes. Add cooked , prepared chicken and stir. Mixture will be thick.

Add cheese (your choice)-on top of each bowl with a little sour cream.

***so satisfying!!

Mom's Hot Dog Soup

1 lg. onion-chopped
1-16oz. pkg. hot dog-cut sliced bite size
1-13 oz. can tomato sauce
2-14.5 0z. cans chicken broth
1-15 oz. can sweet peas-drained
½ cup orzo
¼ tsp. garlic powder
2 tbsp. butter
salt and pepper to taste

Cook orzo as directed, drain and set aside.

Sauté onions in 1 tbsp. butter .Add hot dogs and cook till slightly golden. Add salt and pepper .Add the chicken broth, peas, tomato sauce, 1 cup water and garlic powder. Simmer for a minute or two.

Add the cooked orzo and stir . Allow to cook a few minutes for the orzo to absorb the flavors.

Add butter and stir

*****My favorite childhood lunch!!

Lentil Soup

1 onion- chopped
¼ cup olive oil
2 carrots-small dice
2 celery stalks-chopped
1 clove garlic-minced
1 tsp. dry oregano
3 tbsp. vinegar
Romano cheese

1 bay leaf
1-14.5 0z. Can crushed tomatoes
2 cups dry lentils
8 cups water
½ cup spinach--washed and chopped
   (frozen can be used)
salt and pepper to taste
1 bunch scallions-chopped

In a lg. soup pot ---

Heat oil-over medium heat- add onions, carrots, and celery. Cook until
tender.
Add garlic, bay leaf, and oregano. Stir well. Cook for about 4 minutes.

Add lentils and stir. Add water and tomatoes . Bring to a boil and reduce
heat. Simmer for about 1 hour. Stir occasionally- till lentils are tender.

Just before serving add spinach and cook for another 5 minutes-on low heat.
Stir in vinegar, salt and pepper to taste.

*** add more vinegar according to taste
Sprinkle with Romano cheese and scallions on top of each bowl.

Cabbage and Hamburg Soup

1 lg. onion-chopped
1 lb. Hamburg
1-16 0z.can diced tomatoes- with liquid
3 tbsp. fresh parsley-chopped
2 small garlic cloves-crushed
2 cups water
½ cup grated parmesan cheese
8 cups chicken broth
salt and pepper to taste
3 tbsp. margarine
1 lg. can tomato sauce
1 head cabbage--diced

Sautee onions and Hamburg in margarine. (Pull Hamburg apart and cook
thoroughly.)
Add tomatoes, parsley and garlic. Simmer for 10 minutes and add cabbage.
Mix well.
Cover and simmer for 20 minutes-stirring occasionally. Add broth, salt and
pepper, tomato sauce and water.
Cover and simmer for 1 hour.

Sprinkle in the parmesan cheese and serve.

Avgolémono----- Greek Egg Lemon Soup

6 eggs
1-¼ cups long grain rice
salt and pepper
4 cans chicken broth --or stock
1-¼ cups lemon juice-or less to taste

In a lg. soup pot add chicken broth, salt and pepper and enough water to equal 6 quarts. Bring to a boil. Add rice and bring back to a slow boil and cook till tender. -about 20 minutes. Shut off heat.

In a lg. bowl beat eggs with electric mixer till frothy for about 3 minutes. Slowly drizzle in lemon juice while beating constantly.

Continue beating while adding small amounts of hot broth from soup pot to eggs and lemon mixture. (to temper eggs to prevent curdling)-about 4 cups

Pour mixture slowly into soup pot. Stir well.

***Add small pieces of cooked chicken to individual bowls. Sprinkle with crumbled Feta cheese. (optional)

MMMMM-SO COMFORTING!

Junk Soup---Family Style

2 lg. onions-chopped

3 celery stalks-lg. dice

3 lg. carrots-lg. dice

3 cans chicken broth

2 lbs. lean ground beef

1 lg. can peeled tomatoes- cut up- with liquid

1 lg. can tomato puree

1-8 oz. can tomato sauce

1 can mushrooms-with liquid

Salt and pepper to taste

1 tsp. onion powder

¾ tsp. garlic salt

3 tbsp. margarine

3 tbsp. Worcestershire sauce

½ tsp. oregano

1 can peas--with liquid

4 cups water

1 can peas

--- 1-½ cups macaroni-cook
and set aside

In a lg. soup pot sauté all veggies till tender and lightly brown. Add ground beef- breaking into pieces and cook well.

Add chicken broth, oregano, Worcestershire sauce, salt and pepper, garlic salt, onion powder, tomatoes, tomato puree, tomato sauce, peas and water. Bring to a boil and lower heat. Add cooked macaroni and stir well.

Simmer for 5 minutes and turn off heat. Add 3 tbsp. margarine and mix.

***If soup is too thick- add more water or broth.

Serve with garlic bread   Serves 6

Corn Chowder

3 lg. potatoes-peeled and cubed
1 lg. onion- chopped
1-¼ cups water
¼ cup butter or margarine
2 can creamed corn
2 cans whole kernel corn-with liquid
3 cups whole milk
1 cup ½ and ½ or cream.
salt and pepper to taste
scallions-finely chopped (for garnish)

In a soup pot sauté onions till tender. Add water , butter, and potatoes.
Simmer until fork tender. Add corn, milk and cream and simmer on low
heat for 15 minutes.
Add salt and pepper to taste. Garnish with finely chopped scallions

Chili

1 lb. ground chuck (or turkey)
½ lb. ground pork
1 lg. onion- chopped
2 green peppers- chopped
1 lg. can peeled tomatoes
1 lg. can stewed tomatoes
1-14 oz. kidney beans-drained
3 tbsp. chili powder
1 tbsp. ground cumin
1 tbsp. red cayenne pepper (or less--optional)
2 stalks celery-chopped
1 tbsp. cocoa powder
Salt and pepper to taste

Sauté ground meat, onions, peppers and celery. Add tomatoes, chili powder,
cumin and cocoa powder. Salt and pepper to taste.
Simmer for 30 minutes and mix well. And cayenne pepper to taste..
 Add kidney beans and simmer for another 30 minutes , covered.
Stir occasionally.

Serves 6-8   ***Sprinkle individual servings with favorite cheese
                                And crusty bread.

                    ***Cayenne pepper is extremely hot---adjust to taste

Tomato Rice Soup with Feta

oil
1 lg. onion-chopped
1 lg. carrot-finely diced
2 cans chicken broth
1-8 0z. can tomato sauce
1-14.5oz can diced tomatoes
salt and pepper to taste
5 cans water
1-¼ cups rice-cooked

Cook rice as directed--set aside.
In a soup pot sauté onions and carrots in a little oil till tender.
Add broth, water, tomato sauce, diced tomatoes, salt and pepper to taste.

Bring pot to a boil and lower heat. Add cooked rice and cook on low heat
another 3-4 minutes.
Turn off heat and add 2 tbsp. butter or margarine and stir.

***Sprinkle Feta cheese in each serving bowl. (optional)

Fassolátha-----Bean Soup with Hot Peppers

1 lb. Great Northern beans
water
1 cup olive oil
salt and pepper
1 tbsp. tomato paste
2 carrots-sliced
1 lg. potato- peeled and cubed
3 stalks celery-chopped
2 small hot red peppers- to taste--(optional)
1 lg. onion-diced

Soak beans in warm water overnight.
Drain and rinse beans and place in soup pot. Add enough water to cover beans.
Bring to a boil and cook for 5 minutes-- and drain.

Refill pot with enough water to cover beans by 2 inches. Add oil, salt and pepper, tomato paste, carrots, potatoes, celery, onions and hot peppers.

Bring to a boil, reduce heat, cover and simmer on low heat for about 1 hour and 45 minutes.
Beans should be soft and creamy. Cook longer if necessary.

***Serve with a Greek salad and enjoy!

Greek Interpretations

Psomia----- Breads
Orektika--- Appetizers
Mezedes---Tiny Appetizers
Salates ---- Salads
Krasia------Wines
Liker------- Liqueurs
Pota--------- Alcohol Drinks
Pagota------Ice Cream
Frouta------ Fruit
Epidorpia-- Desserts
Makaronades-Spaghetti
Pastes----- Pastries
Glyka----- Sweets, Pastry,Candy
Ouzo----- Alcoholic Drink--Anise
Retsina--- White or Rose wine
Soupes---- Soups
Hortarika--Veggies
Prota Piata-Entrees
Kreatika---Meat Dishes
Poulerika---- Poultry Dishes
Psaria--------- Fish
Thalassina-- Seafood
Kynigia----- Game

NOTES***

Cooking with garlic, herbs, spices, lemons, Greek cheeses, Greek olive oil, and Greek olives are crucial ingredients in Greek cooking -which gives Greek food It's unique, distinct and magical flavors.

KALI OREXI-----GOOD APPETITE !!!

Salads

Salads

Chilled Orzo Salad
Lenten Salad
Summer Noodle Salad
Crispy Bacon and Bean Salad
Creamy Macaroni Salad
Pasta Salad--- with a Greek Touch
Basil Salad
Stuffed Tomato Salad
Lima Bean Salad
Greek Salad
So Fruity Salad Delight
Macaroni and Cheese Salad
Cranberry Salad Delight
Sweet Potato Salad
Mavromátika Fasólia Saláta------Black -Eyed Pea Salad
Cucumber Yogurt Salad
Veggie Salad Surprise
Crab and Olive Salad
Festive Fruit Salad
Spinach and Feta Salad

Chilled Orzo Salad

1 cup orzo
1 can cut green beans-drained
¼ cup red peppers-chopped
1 cup tomatoes--seeded and finely chopped
½ cup onions-chopped
1 tsp. garlic-minced
salt and pepper to taste
3 tsp. olive oil
½ cup feta cheese-crumbled
2 tsp. lemon juice

Cook orzo according to directions.

In a lg. bowl--mix all remaining ingredients . After orzo has cooled for a
few minutes-mix with the vegetables. Stir well.
Season to taste and chill before serving.

****This dish will please everyone.**

Lenten Salad

6 hard boiled eggs
8 anchovies
¼ cup mayonnaise or salad dressing
tomato wedges
1 cup celery-diced
¼ tsp. salt
pinch of pepper
lettuce
Greek olives
½ small onion- or scallions-chopped

Slice the eggs and chop anchovies.
Combine with celery, onions, mayonnaise, or salad dressing, salt and pepper.
Serve on a bed of lettuce with tomato wedges and Greek olives.

***A great addition to a Lenten meal---or enjoy any time--

Summer Noodle Salad

5-½ to 6 cups egg noodles
3 quarts boiling water
salt and pepper
2 cups apples--peeled and diced
1 cup grated carrot
½ cup sweet pickles--chopped
½ small onion-grated
½ cup mayonnaise (or more)
½ cup sour cream
1 can mandarin oranges--drained

Add ½ tsp. salt to boiling water.
Add noodles-continue to boil uncovered till tender. Stir occasionally
and drain. Rinse very briefly with cold water.

**In a lg. bowl--

Toss noodles with carrots, apples, onions, pickles, and oranges.
Blend in sour cream and mayonnaise. Add salt and pepper to taste.
Chill in fridge for several hours before serving.

***Serves 8-10

****An added attraction to a picnic!

Crispy Bacon and Bean Salad

½ cup salad oil
2/3 cup vinegar
½ cup sugar
salt and pepper
1 onion-chopped
1 cup bacon bits
1 can cut green beans
1 can wax beans
1 can lima beans
1 lg. tomato-finely diced

In a bowl---
Whisk oil, vinegar, sugar, salt and pepper together. Pour over
all ingredients and mix well.

***Quick and easy!!

Creamy Macaroni Salad

½ lb. elbow macaroni-cooked
4 hard boiled eggs-sliced
2 stalks celery--slice lengthwise and chop
1 small red onion-minced
½ cup pimento olives--diced
½ cup (or more) mayonnaise
1/8 cup cream
¼ cup vinegar
salt and pepper to taste
½ cucumber-chopped
1 carrot-diced

Put all veggies in a bowl.

Combine mayonnaise, salt and pepper, vinegar, cream and whisk till well incorporated.
Pour over salad and mix well.

***A great change from the every day salad!

Pasta Salad----With A Greek Touch

½ cup olive oil
½ cup red wine vinegar
salt and pepper
¾ tsp. sugar
2 cups mushrooms
1 bunch cherry tomatoes--halved
1 cup red bell peppers- sliced
½ cup green onions-chopped
pepperoni sausages--sliced

1 tsp. garlic powder
1 tsp dried basil
2-½ cups elbow macaroni--
(cooked)
1 cup feta cheese-crumbled
1 can black olives-sliced
1 tsp. oregano

Whisk together the olive oil, vinegar, garlic powder, basil, oregano, salt and pepper, and sugar.

Add pasta, mushrooms, tomatoes, red peppers, feta cheese, green onions, olives and peppers.
Mix together well.

***Serve chilled--with crusty bread and a glass of wine!

****A great addition to a meal for guests!!   Makes an exciting lunch meal!!

Basil Salad

½ head lettuce-washed and dried
1 cucumber-with skin - cut in thin, diagonal slices
6 radishes-washed and sliced

Break lettuce into bite size pieces.
Put in a serving bowl or on a platter

Place cucumber slices around the outer edge of the platter.
Place the radishes over the center portion of the lettuce.

** Dressing---

¼ cup white vinegar
2 tbsp. basil
2 pkgs. Equal
¼ cup water (optional)

Whisk altogether and pour evenly over the salad.

**   Serves 4

***A delightful change ! Serve with your favorite cheeses.

Stuffed Tomato Salad

4 medium sized tomatoes
2 potatoes- boiled
6 green olives
3 anchovy fillets
1 tbsp. parsley-chopped
2 tbsp. olive oil
2 tbsp. red wine vinegar
salt and pepper to taste
1 green pepper -chopped

Wash tomatoes. Cut a thin slice off the top. (stem side)
Scoop out seeds and pulp. Sprinkle inside of tomatoes with a pinch of salt.

Cut boiled potatoes in cubes. Cut olives and anchovies in small pieces.

Add parsley, oil, vinegar, salt and pepper. Mix altogether.
Stuff tomatoes with mixture.
Garnish the top with an olive and chopped peppers.

****Serve on lettuce leaves

Lima Bean Salad

2-½ cups lima beans
1 lg. onion-chopped
1/3 cup olive oil
juice of 1 lemon
salt and pepper to taste

**Cook lima beans till tender and drain.

In a lg. bowl--

Add beans, chopped onions, salt and pepper, olive oil and lemon juice.
Toss well.
   ***Serve warm or cold

      ***Simple and so tasty!!

Greek Salad

1 green pepper-sliced
1 head lettuce- break apart with your hands
3 tomatoes-cut bite size pieces
1 cucumber-peeled and sliced
1 bunch scallions--chopped-use the whites
salt and pepper to taste
¼ lb. feta cheese-crumbled
x-tra virgin olive oil
red wine vinegar
1 lg. red onion- sliced in thin rings
1 tsp. dried oregano
2 stalks celery-chopped
capers (optional)
12 Kalamata olives
Anchovies (optional)

Combine all ingredients in a lg. bowl except the oil and vinegar.
Toss well.

Combine oil , vinegar , salt and pepper and whisk thoroughly . Pour over
salad and mix well.
Crumble the feta cheese all over top.

***Greek salads have many different versions.
This one is delicious--**Try it!

So Fruity Salad Delight

Wash and cut all fruit to your desired size---

assorted cheeses--your favorites
crusty Italian bread - cut into cubes
2 oranges-peeled
2 apples peeled
2 peaches
strawberries
blueberries
melon balls--cantelope and honeydew
watermelon balls
grapes-halved--red and white
apricots-halved
2 key limes-sliced
2 bananas-peeled, sliced

***Add bananas at the last minute to preserve color.**

Toss all fruit and bread together.

**3 choices for the dressing-----

#1---beaten cream with mayonnaise
#2---a light, sweetened French dressing
#3---yogurt-plain or flavored --and a little sour cream

*****Serve as is---or over lettuce wedges, with plain yogurt- or cottage cheese

***This is delightfully refreshing!!

Macaroni and Cheese Salad

2 cups macaroni-cooked and drained
1-12 oz. can chopped or baked ham - cut into chunks
1 cup sharp cheddar cheese- cubed
½ cup celery-chopped
½ cup green onions- with tops- sliced
2 tbsp. pimento -chopped
¼ cup pickle relish
½ cup mayonnaise
1 tbsp. mustard
salt and pepper to taste

Combine first 7 ingredients-.

In a bowl--
Blend mayonnaise , mustard, salt and pepper. Add to ingredients
And mix well.
   Chill in fridge-Serve on lettuce with tomato wedges on the side.

***Serve with any meal or as a meal by itself--

 ****Wonderful cookout accompaniment !!

Cranberry Salad Delight

1 pkg. orange flavored gelatin
1 cup boiling water
½ cup cold water
1 tbsp. lemon juice
1-14 0z jar cranberry orange relish
2 tbsp. crystallized ginger
1-5 oz. can water chestnuts--drained and chopped
½ tsp. celery seeds

Dissolve gelatin in boiling water. Add cold water and lemon juice.
Mix well.
Chill until it begins to thicken.

Fold in relish, ginger, watercress and celery seeds.
Pour into individual molds and chill.

****Refreshing!!   Great as a dessert or side dish!

Sweet Potato Salad

2 cups sweet potatoes- cooked, cooled and salted
1-½ cups celery-diced
2 cups apples-diced
1 cup orange sections
1 cup salted peanuts-chopped
cooked fruit dressing--can use jam or jelly
water cress

Combine potatoes, celery, apples, oranges and nuts.
Moisten well with dressing.

Serve on a bed of watercress.

***Great with any meal**

Mavromátika Fasólia Saláta-------Black Eyed Pea Salad

2-10 oz. pkgs. frozen black eyed peas
1 lg. red onion -slice very thin
¼ cup olive oil
2 tbsp. wine vinegar
2 tbsp. parsley-chopped

Cook peas as directed on pkg. and drain.
Combine with onions, olive oil, and vinegar.

Sprinkle with chopped parsley.
   Chill before serving.

Serves 4

Cucumber-Yogurt Salad

3 tbsp. olive oil
1 tbsp. vinegar
2 cloves garlic-chopped
salt and pepper to taste
1 cup plain yogurt
1 cup sour cream
2 lg. cucumbers-peeled, seeded, and diced
1 tsp. fresh dill

In a bowl- combine olive oil, vinegar, garlic, salt and pepper.
Whisk well.--

In a separate bowl--
Blend together the yogurt and sour cream.
Combine this with the oil mixture.
Add cucumbers and mix well.
    Chill in fridge.

Sprinkle with dill before serving.

  ****Use as a dip or serve on a bed of lettuce with sliced tomatoes.

Veggie Salad Surprise

1 cup red cabbage- finely chopped
1 cup green cabbage-f finely chopped
1 cup curly endive- chopped
1 cup lettuce- finely chopped
2 zucchini- slice thin
1-½ cup cauliflowerets -chopped
1 small onion-finely sliced

3 tbsp. wine vinegar
8 tbsp. salad oil
½ cup sour cream
8 anchovies fillets
½ cup Roquefort cheese
   (crumbled)
1 tsp. sugar
¼ tsp. mustard
salt and pepper to taste

In a lg. bowl---
Combine first 7 ingredients from left column.

In a small bowl mix sugar, mustard, salt, pepper and vinegar.
Add oil slowly to sour cream and beat until smooth.

Blend with vinegar mixture.
Pour dressing over salad and toss lightly. Cut anchovie fillets into small
pieces and sprinkle on top along with crumbled cheese.

****Serve with garlic bread! ----A meal in itself!

Crab and Olive Salad

1-13 oz. can crabmeat
2/3 cup ripe olives-chopped
Romaine lettuce
1-2/3 cup celery-- small dice
¼ cup mayonnaise --or salad dressing
salt and pepper to taste

Separate the crabmeat removing bits of bone.
Combine with olives, celery, and mayonnaise- or salad dressing.
Season with salt and pepper, Place on a bed of lettuce and tomato wedges

***enjoy!!

Festive Fruit Salad

1 lg. container cottage cheese
1 box orange jello
1 lg. can mandarin oranges
1 lg. can crushed pineapple
1 lg. container whipped cream

Drain oranges and pineapples well. ---set aside
Save some of the oranges for decoration.

***In a lg. bowl--
Combine cottage cheese and dry jello mix until well blended.
Stir in pineapple and mix well. Gently stir in mandarin oranges

Fold in whipped cream until everything is blended together.

Pour into a 13x9 glass baking dish. Arrange remaining oranges on top in a
pattern.

Refrigerate for several hours or over night is best.

    ***cool and refreshing!

Spinach and Feta Salad

3 onions-chopped
2 tomatoes-diced
1 cucumber sliced
¼ cup fresh lemon juice
1 tbsp. mild mustard
1/3 cup red wine vinegar
2 lbs. raw spinach
salt and pepper to taste
¾ cup olive oil
½ lb. Feta cheese-crumbled

Wash spinach, drain well .(wipe off with paper towels)
Remove all stems. Slice spinach and place in salad bowl.
Add cucumbers , tomatoes, feta cheese and onions. Mix well.

In a separate bowl-- combine olive oil, lemon juice, mustard, salt, pepper
and vinegar. Whisk until well incorporated.
Pour dressing over salad and mix well.

***A variety of cheeses used in Greek cuisine include Feta, Kasseri,
Kefalotyri, Graviera, Anthotyros, Manouri, Metsovone and Mizithra.

Ingredient Substitutions

Ingredient	Amount	Substitution
Allspice	1 tsp.	½ tsp. cinnamon+ ½ tsp. clove
Apple Pie spice	1 tsp.	½ tsp.cinnamon,¼ tsp. nutmeg +1/8 tsp. cardamom
Baking powder	1 tsp.	1/3 tsp. baking soda+ ½ tsp. cream of tartar
Bread	1 slice	¾ cup bread crumbs
Broth	1 cup	1 bullion cube
Buttermilk	1 cup	1 cup plain yogurt
Coconut cream	1 cup	1 cup whipping cream
Coconut milk	1 cup	1 cup whole milk
Corn	1 dozen ears	2-½ cups cooked corn
Corn syrup	1 cup	1-¼ cups light brown sugar +½ cup water
Corn starch	1 tbsp.	2 tbsp. all purpose flour
Cracker crumbs	¾ cup	1 cup dry bread crumbs
Eggs, uncooked	1 cup	5 lg. eggs
Flour	1 cup	1-½ cups rolled oats
Parsley-dried	1 tsp.	3 tsp. fresh chopped parsley
Shortening-melted-1 cup		1 cup cookng oil
Sour cream	1 cup	1 cup plain yogurt
Sugar-brown	1 cup	1 cup granulated sugar
Tomato Juice	1 cup	1½ cup tomato sauce+½ cup water
Worcestershire sauce	1 tsp.	1 tsp. steak sauce
Yogurt-plain	1 cup	1 cup sour cream

Sauces and Dips

Sauces and Dips

Cucumber sauce for Salmon
Sweet and Sour Sauce
Dill Sauce
Bread Loaf Dip
Spinach Dip
Veggie Dip
Tooty Fruity Dip
Cheddar and Bacon Spread
Raisin Sauce -With a Sweet Touch
Crabmeat Spread
Bleu Cheese Balls
Chinese Chicken Wings
Crab Ravigote
Rumaki
Taco Dip
Béchamel Sauce
Diet Dressing (with great flavor)
Lemon Sauce for Grilled Fish
Tartar Sauce
Tzatziki (Traditional Cucumber and Garlic Sauce)
Lemon Butter Sauce
Skordalia (Greek Potato and Garlic Dip)
Cream Cheese Salsa Dip
Hot Crabmeat Dip

Cucumber Sauce For Salmon

1 large cucumber
1/3 cup sour cream
1/3 cup mayonnaise
1-½ tsp. dried dill
¼ tsp. salt
1/8 tsp. pepper
Dash of hot pepper sauce

Peel, seed and shred cucumber.
Press out moisture with a paper towel.
Combine sour cream, mayonnaise, dill, salt and pepper and hot pepper sauce.
Mix well

Chill for several hours before serving
Brush on both sides of fish.
Cook fish as directed

Sweet and Sour Sauce

1 cup water
½ cup white vinegar
½ cup sugar
½ cup tomato paste
5 tsp. corn starch

Mix all ingredients together in a sauce pan.
Bring to a boil. Reduce to medium heat stirring constantly.
Cook for 1-2 minutes more.

Dill Sauce

1-1/2 cups mayonnaise
1 lemon-juiced
salt and pepper to taste
1 tbsp. dill-dried
2 tbsp. extra virgin olive oil

Whisk the mayonnaise, and olive oil together until smooth.
Add the dill, lemon juice, salt and pepper. Whisk again.

Allow to chill for 2 hours before serving.

* If consistency is too thick ,add a little more oil and lemon juice.
Pour over cooked salmon or any favorite fish .

Bread Loaf Dip

1 cup mayonnaise
1 cup sour cream
1 cup cream cheese
1 cup pimento olives- minced
1 tsp. dill

1 round loaf sweet bread
1 loaf French or Italian bread

Hollow out middle of both breads and cut up into bite size chunks.
Mix the dip ingredients together. Pour dip into one hollowed out bread. .
Place loaf on a serving platter with bread chunks all around.

* SO GOOD!!!

Spinach Dip

1 pkg. frozen spinach---thawed, cooked drain and chop
1-½ cups sour cream
½ cup mayonnaise
¾ pkg. Knore's vegetable soup

Mix all ingredients together
Chill and serve

Veggie Dip

1 cup mayonnaise
1 cup sour cream
1 tbsp. mustard
Salt and pepper to taste
1 onion- finely chopped
2 garlic cloves- finely chopped

Combine all ingredients, chill and serve

* recipe can easily be doubled

Tooty Fruity Dip

1 pkg. instant vanilla pudding
1 cup milk
1-8 oz. vanilla yogurt
1 can pineapples-drained
1 cup strawberries-sliced   Any fruit will do--
1 cup blueberries

Mix pudding and milk. Add yogurt and mix again.
If mixture is too thick, add a little more milk.

* Chill and serve with your favorite fruit variety.

Cheddar and Bacon Spread

10 oz. extra sharp cheddar cheese
4 bacon slices- cooked crispy and drained
½ cup milk
¼ cup mayonnaise
1 tsp. Worcestershire sauce
1/8 tsp. red pepper
Small bunch chives-chopped

Fry the bacon till crisp and drain on a paper towel. Shred the cheese.

Put the cheese, milk, mayonnaise, Worcestershire sauce and red pepper in a blender and mix till smooth. Add bacon and blend together.

Pour into a bowl and sprinkle chives on top.

* Serve with veggies or crusty bread

Raisin Sauce---With a Sweet Touch

1-15 0z. Box seedless raisins
1 cup sugar
2 cups water
¼ tsp. cinnamon

Cook raisins in water till soft and falling apart. Add cinnamon
(do not drain liquid)

To make Syrup---

Mix together 1 cup sugar, 1 cup water, and cook until sugar is well dissolved.

Then add syrup mixture to raisins. Simmer for about 30 minutes, stirring occasionally.

*If sauce is too thick, add a little more water. If too thin, add a little corn starch.

This is delicious over ham!

Crabmeat Spread

1-8oz. Pkg. cream cheese -softened
1 can crabmeat-drained and check for bones
cocktail sauce
¼ tsp. onion pdr.

Mix the cream cheese with the crabmeat. Put into the serving bowl and chill until ready to serve.
Just before serving spread cocktail sauce over the top.

Serve with party bread slices or crackers.

Bleu Cheese Balls

1-8 oz. pkg. cream cheese-softened
1-4 oz. pkg. bleu cheese-softened
¼ cup margarine-softened
¼ cup ripe olives-chopped
¼ cup green pepper-chopped
1 tsp. garlic salt
1/3 cup walnuts- chopped

Blend cheese and margarine. Add all other ingredients and mix well.
Shape into balls and roll in nuts. Chill and serve with crackers.

Chinese Chicken Wings

2 pkgs. Chicken wings--average size
2 beef bullion cubes
1 tsp. garlic pdr.
4 tbsp. soy sauce
1 pinch of ginger
2 cups boiling water

Mix above ingredients and pour over the chicken wings. Refrigerate
For at least 24 hours.

Put wings in a shallow pan and bake @ 350 deg. For 50-60 minutes

Crab Ravigote

1 can crab meat
1 hard boiled egg-chopped extra fine
½ tsp. mustard
1 tsp. capers- mashed
2 tsp. lemon juice
mayonnaise- enough to bind

Mix all ingredients well, and chill. Place in pastry shells . To serve, add a slice of pimento for garnish.

Great as a dip with crackers.

Rumaki

chicken livers
water chestnuts-sliced
bacon
Onion powder
Pepper

Cut chicken livers into bite size pieces. Wrap each one with a slice of bacon
and a water chestnut. Secure with a wooden toothpick.
Season with onion powder and pepper.

Broil, turning them every few minutes until bacon is crispy and liver is
cooked through.

Taco Dip

1 lb. Hamburg
1 pkg. Taco dry seasoning mix
1 container sour cream
chopped lettuce
chopped tomatoes
1 jar Taco sauce-mild or hot
1 small onion -chopped
shredded mozzarella cheese

Brown the Hamburg in a skillet. Add the onion and cook till tender. Add the seasoning mix with water (use directions on pkg.)

Simmer until liquid is absorbed. Using an 8-or 9 inch deep serving dish, layer the sour cream, Hamburg mixture, chopped lettuce, chopped tomatoes, shredded Mozzarella cheese and Taco sauce----and serve

Béchamel Sauce   (White Sauce)

4 cups milk (must be hot)
6 tbsp. flour
4 tbsp. butter
3 tbsp. grated cheese
1 tsp. salt
½ tsp. grated nutmeg

Melt butter in saucepan. Add flour gradually, stirring constantly with a wire beater until all the butter is absorbed.
Add the hot milk slowly and stir until it thickens and starts boiling.

Add salt and nutmeg and continue stirring until sauce becomes smooth and thick and creamy.

Add the grated cheese and allow to boil a few more minutes.

Diet Dressing (with great flavor)

½ cup salad oil
¼ cup lemon juice
¼ cup water
½ tsp salt
 ½ cup ketchup
1 tsp dry mustard
¼ tsp paprika
½ tsp Worcestershire sauce

Combine all ingredients. Beat until well incorporated. Place in jar with tight lid and chill. Shake well before using.

* can be used for salads and meats--

Lemon Sauce for Grilled Fish

2 lbs. fish (your choice)
1 cup oil
2 tbsp. parsley- chopped
1 tsp. mustard
2 tbsp. water
Salt and pepper to taste

Grill the fish--

Beat all the ingredients together and pour over the grilled fish and serve.

(Easy but delicious)

Tartar Sauce

½ cup mayonnaise
½ tsp. spicy brown mustard
2 tsp. sweet pickles- finely chopped
½ tsp. capers (drained and chopped)
1 tsp. lemon juice
1 tsp. onion- finely chopped

Combine all ingredients and chill before serving--

Tzatziki-- (Traditional Yogurt Cucumber and Garlic Sauce)

1 container plain yogurt
½ cup sour cream
4 cucumbers-peel, remove seeds and shred
3 cloves garlic- peeled and minced
Salt and pepper to taste
1 tbsp. olive oil

Drain yogurt in cheese cloth over night. (do not put in fridge.)
Drain cucumbers till liquid stops running.
 Mix together.

In a small bowl mash the garlic with the olive oil.
Stir in salt, pepper, cucumbers, yogurt and sour cream.

Cover and chill for at least 1 hour or more.

* Spread on garlic bread or use as a dip for crackers and raw veggies.

Lemon Butter Sauce

½ cup margarine or butter- melted
½ tsp salt
Pepper to taste
¼ cup lemon juice
2 tbsp. parsley-minced

Combine all ingredients. Heat in saucepan for about 2 minutes.
Stir well to blend.

Skordalia   (Greek Potato and Garlic Dip)

4 garlic cloves-mashed
1 tsp. salt
1 egg yolk--keep the white
3 tbsp. vinegar
1 cup salad oil
5 potatoes -cook in salted water and mash
Pepper to taste

Put the garlic and salt in a bowl and mash together.
Add egg yolk and vinegar .

Beat until well incorporated. Add oil and alternate with hot
Mashed potatoes. Add pepper to taste. Mix until smooth.

* If mixture is too thick add some of the egg white--

Serve as a dip, condiment or with fish or meat

Cream Cheese Salsa Dip

1 jar veggie salsa
1 - 8 oz. container sour cream
1-16 oz. container plain cream cheese (at room temp)
1 lg. bag Craft 4 cheese blend

Mix together the sour cream, and cream cheese.
Spread it evenly on bottom of serving dish.

Then spread out the salsa and sprinkle all the cheese on top.

* Serve with dip chips, crackers or veggie pieces

Hot Crabmeat Dip

8 0z pkg. cream cheese
1 tsp. cream or half and half
6-½ oz. can flaked crabmeat
2 tsp. onion- minced
½ tsp. horseradish
¼ tsp. salt and a dash of pepper

Combine all ingredients. Pour into baking dish and sprinkle with 1/3 cup slivered almonds.

Bake @ 375 deg. For 15 minutes

Fresh Vegetable Cooking Reference for Steaming--

Cooking time varies slightly with the size and amount of veggies.

Artichokes---------------25-30 minutes
Asparagus   ------------10-12min.
Beans-Green-------------20-30min.
Beans Lima--------------25-30 min.
Beets---------------------30-40 min.
Broccoli----------------- 8-15 min.
Brussels Sprouts------ - 12 min.
Cabbage-cut in quarters-15-20 min.
Carrots-sliced---------- 10-15 min.
Cauliflower- whole----15-20 min.
Celery-pieces-----------15-20 min.
Corn on the Cob---------12-20 min.
Eggplant-----------------15-18 min.
Leeks -------------- ---- 8-10 min.
Mushrooms------------- 5-8 min.
Okra -------------------- 25-30 min.
Onions -whole ------ 25-30 min.
Parsnips -------------- 8-12 min.
Peas   --------------- 5-8 min.
Potatoes --whole------ 15-30 min.
Spinach ------------- 5-8-mn.
Squash   sliced ------- 8-10 min.
Swiss Chard ---------10-15 min.
Tomatoes ------------ 2-3 min.
Turnip -whole ------ 20-25 min.
Zucchini   ---------- 5-10 min.

*** Vegetables are a generous source of all essential vitamins and minerals vital to good health.
Cook them in as little water as possible when steaming. This will give you the best result for your effort.--Steaming begins at the boiling point!!!

Side Dishes

Side Dishes

Zucchini Bake
Stuffing for Chicken or Turkey
Lima Beans Plaki
Spanahorizo----Spinach and Rice
Orzo and Spinach Bake with Cheese
Lemon and Basil Rice
Summer Squash Casserole
Greek Style Potatoes
Herb Roasted Potatoes
Kolokythokeftedes----Zucchini, Cheese and herb Fritters
Classic Corn Bread
Greek Potato Salad
Potato Casserole
Rice Pilaf
Orzo Stuffed Mushrooms
Southern Style Potato Bake
Feta Cheese Eggplant Parmesan
Oven Roasted Veggies
Pan Fried Brussels Sprouts
Sweet Baked Squash

Zucchini Bake

1 clove garlic-minced
4 small zucchini-sliced thin
1 cup Feta cheese- crumbled
1 cup cheddar cheese- grated
½ cup onions- chopped
pinch of parsley, dill and mint
¼ cup mushrooms- sliced (optional)
4 eggs-beaten
1 cup Bisquick mix
¼ cup olive oil

Mix together the zucchini, garlic, Feta cheese, cheddar cheese, onions, parsley, dill, and mint, and mushrooms.

Beat together--
Eggs, olive oil, Bisquick, and add to squash mixture. Stir till well blended. Bake @ 350deg. For 45 minutes.

Stuffing for turkey or chicken

2 lbs. Hamburg
3 tbsp. butter
1 lg. onion- chopped
8 lg. potatoes- peeled and diced
Salt and pepper to taste
2 cloves garlic-finely chopped
1 tsp. mint

Cook potatoes in separate pot, drain , mash and set aside.
Sauté onions and garlic in butter .Add Hamburg -cook till well done.
Add salt, pepper and mint. Cook for a few more minutes. Remove from heat .

Add Hamburg mixture, with liquid to mashed potatoes. Mix well.
Reseason if necessary.

* Great with any food---can be made the day before.

Lima Beans Plaki

1 lb. lima beans
½ cup olive oil
3 onions- chopped
2 cloves garlic- finely minced
1 cup dry white wine
3 carrots-thinly sliced
3 celery stalks -diced
1 green pepper- diced
1-16 oz. can tomato sauce
½ cup parsley- finely chopped
1 bay leaf
1 tbsp. fresh dill- finely chopped
1 tsp. dry basil
1 tsp. sugar
Salt and pepper to taste

Soak lima beans over night. Change water and boil in 10 cups of water, till tender.

In a heavy skillet, heat oil and sauté chopped onions. till soft and transparent. Add minced garlic and sauté 1 or 2 minutes. Add wine, carrots, celery and green pepper. Reduce heat, cover and allow to simmer for 10 minutes.

Remove cover and stir in tomato sauce, parsley bay leaf, dill and sugar. Add salt and pepper. Cover sauce and simmer for 30 minutes.
(or until the veggies are tender)

Drain lima beans (reserving the liquid) and add to sauce with 1 cup of reserved liquid. (sauce should not be too dry) Simmer over low heat for 15-20 minutes. --Add a little more liquid if necessary.

Serve hot or cold with Feta cheese ,black Greek olives and crusty bread.

   *   Keeps well in fridge for 1 week.

Spanahorizo---Spinach and Rice

½ cup olive oil
Parsley-1 bunch-finely chopped
2 cups water
1 lg. onion- chopped
2 tbsp. tomato paste
Salt and pepper to taste
2 chicken bouillon cubes
1 can chicken broth
1 small can tomato sauce
1 can chopped tomatoes
2 bags fresh spinach chopped and remove stems
1 cup rice- uncooked

Heat oil in in lg. saucepan. Sauté onions till tender. Add parsley, water, chicken broth, and bouillon cubes. Bring to a boil.
Add tomato paste, tomato sauce, chopped tomatoes, salt and pepper. Mix together thoroughly.

Add spinach and rice -stir well. Simmer on lower heat for about 30 minutes or until rice is done. Stir occasionally-don't allow rice to stick.

Allow to sit before serving so that all the liquid can be absorbed.

* If needed, add a little more water while cooking.

Orzo and Spinach Bake with Cheese

2 shallots - chopped
3 tbsp. oil
Salt and pepper to taste
1 tsp. parsley-chopped
1 garlic clove- finely chopped
1 cup orzo
1 cup grated cheddar cheese
1 pkg. frozen spinach -thawed and drained well
1 cup water
2 cups chicken broth

Cook shallots in oil , add garlic, parsley, salt and pepper. Mix well.
Then add the spinach and continue to cook for a few more minutes.

Add the chicken broth, water and orzo. Stir well.

Put in baking pan and bake at 350 deg. For 35 to 40 minutes.

Lemon Basil Rice

½ tsp. basil
½ lemon-juiced
1 cup cheddar cheese
1-¼ cups rice
1 onion-chopped
½ cup green pepper-diced
½ cup celery-diced
1 can whole tomatoes with liquid
1 medium can tomato sauce
1 cup chicken broth

Sauté onions, green pepper, and celery in butter until golden brown. Add salt and pepper, basil and whole tomatoes.

Transfer to a greased casserole dish.
Add rice, tomato sauce, lemon and broth. Slowly mix in ½ the cheese.
Mix well.

Sprinkle remaining cheese on top. Bake covered at 350 deg. For 20minutes.
Uncover and continue to bake till rice is tender.

* Put under broiler for a minute-or so to brown off the cheese. (watch not to burn) optional.

Yummy!!!!!!!

Summer Squash Casserole

1 small pkg. stuffing mix
3-4 summer squash -with peel--boil for 5 minutes and slice
1 stick butter or margarine
1 can cream of celery soup (no water)
1-1 lb container sour cream
1 med. Onion-minced
Salt and pepper to taste

Melt butter in pan. Add ½ pkg. of stuffing and mix well.
Fold in cooked squash ,onion, salt and pepper.

 Topping---

Mix together the soup and sour cream. Pour on top of squash mixture
Top off with remaining dry stuffing mix. Pour into baking dish.
Bake @ 350deg. For 30-40 min utes

Greek Style Potatoes

½ cup olive oil
1-½ cup water
2 cloves garlic-finely chopped
½ cup lemon juice
1 tsp. thyme-dried
½ tsp. rosemary
Salt and pepper to taste
6 large potatoes- peeled and quartered
1 cup chicken broth

Pre-heat oven--350 deg.

Mix together the oil, garlic, water, lemon juice, thyme, rosemary, chicken broth, salt and pepper.

Spread potatoes out on a baking sheet pan.
Pour mixture over potatoes-mix well.
Bake , covered for 1 to 1-½ hours until tender. Uncover and brown.

Herb Roasted Potatoes

2 lg. potatoes--per person
Olive oil (enough to coat potatoes)
Salt and pepper to taste
¾ tsp. rosemary
1 tsp. onion powder or flakes
1 tsp. garlic salt
¼ cup melted butter

Wash potatoes and thoroughly dry them. Cut into quarters. and put in lg. bowl.
Add enough olive oil to coat the potatoes. Season with salt, pepper, onion flakes, garlic salt and rosemary. Mix well to completely cover the potatoes.

Cover with foil and allow to sit for 15 minutes. (gives it more flavor)
Then uncover , mix well and place potatoes on a baking sheet.

Bake at 350 deg. until tender and light golden brown.
Remove pan from oven and pour melted butter all over top.
Mix again and return to oven for 10 minutes

* Great with chicken and Greek salad

Kolokythokeftedes----Zucchini ,Cheese and Herb Fritters

For Fritters:

4 cups coarsely grated zucchini
2 tsp. salt
1 cup scallions finely chopped
1 cup fresh parsley
½ cup mint-fresh
1 tbsp. oregano-dried
1 cup corn starch
1 cup Kefalotiri or Pecorino cheese
8 oz. plain yogurt
2 cups Safflower oil
pepper

Zucchini Batter:

Stir together zucchini and salt. Allow to sit in a colander for 1 hour to drain.

Mix together remaining fritter ingredients . Season well with pepper. Let mixture stand for 15 minutes.

Heat oil about ¼ inch deep in fry pan. Spoon heaping tbsps. of mixture into oil and fry in small batches without crowding.

Turning fritters till golden brown- about 1 minute .
Transfer fritters with a slotted spoon to paper towels to drain.

* return oil to 350deg. again- between batches.

Serve HOT!!

Classic Corn Bread

1 cup corn flower
1 cup flour
3 tsp. baking powder
½ tsp. salt
1 egg
1 cup milk
¼ cup melted shortening

Sift together the corn meal, flower, baking pdr. And salt.

 In another bowl, beat the egg, add milk and shortening.
Add to dry ingredients-stir just to moisten.
Pour into greased pan 8x8x2
Bake @ 400 deg. For 30 minutes

Greek Potato Salad

1-½ red or white potatoes
5 cups water
1 small Purple onion-cut into rings
½ cucumber-diced
5 cherry tomatoes-halved
1 small clove garlic-minced
¼ cup plain yogurt
2 tbsp. Feta cheese- crumbled
¼ tbsp. oregano-dried
1/8 tsp. rosemary-crushed
1/8 tsp. pepper
4 Greek olives
1 tbsp. fresh, chopped parsley

Boil potatoes until just tender. Drain potatoes and chill. Then cut potatoes into ¾ inch cubes. Combine potatoes, cucumber and tomatoes in a lg. bowl. Set aside--

Chop garlic in food processor , add yogurt ,Feta cheese, oregano and rosemary. Process until smooth.
Add mixture to potatoes. Toss gently -coat completely.
Garnish with parsley , olives and onion rings.
Cover and serve chilled.

Potato Casserole

1 bag (2 lbs.) of tiny hash brown potatoes
1 stick melted butter
1 can -cream of mushrooms soup
1 container sour cream
2 cups shredded cheddar cheese
2 cups Corn flakes

Mix potatoes with ¾ of the melted butter along with the remaining ingredients (except the cereal.) Place in 9x12 baking dish.

Crush corn flakes and add remaining ¼ stick of butter. Sprinkle on top of potatoes. Bake @ 350 deg. For 45minutes to an hour.

Rice Pilaf

1 cup long grain rice
 1 cup chicken broth
1 cup water
Salt and pepper to taste
½ cup butter or margarine

Put chicken broth and water on to boil. Add butter, salt , pepper and rice.
Stir well. Bring to a boil. Lower heat, cover and simmer . Allow to cook for
30 minutes, Stir well with fork to fluff rice.

Orzo Stuffed Mushrooms

Olive oil
8 lg. Portabella mushrooms- wipe clean and cut off stems
1 lg. onion- diced
Salt and pepper
capers
Parmesan cheese
bread crumbs
1 tsp. oregano-dried
1cup sun dried tomatoes
1 cup orzo- cook as directed
1 clove garlic-minced

Cook mushrooms in a small amount of oil for a few minutes.
Chop mushroom stems . Add to a fry pan along with onions, garlic and sun dried tomatoes. Add salt and pepper and capers (amount is optional)

Add cooked orzo. Mix well- then fill mushrooms with mixture, Sprinkle tops with parmesan cheese and bread crumbs.
Broil till golden brown.

Southern Style Potato Bake

4 lg. potatoes-washed , peeled-sliced in wedges
1-½ cup mayonnaise
1 tsp. garlic salt
Pepper to taste
Corn bread mix

Put potatoes in a lg. bowl. Add all ingredients except the corn bread. Mix well.
 Dredge potatoes in corn bread mix. Spread potatoes out on a well greased baking sheet.

Bake @ 350 deg. For 50 minutes

Mmmm good

Feta Cheese Eggplant Parmesan

	Feta cheese
1 clove garlic-minced	½ tsp. parsley

1 clove garlic-minced
1 lg. onion-chopped
2 lg. can pureed tomatoes
2 lg. eggplant- washed and sliced in ¼ inch rounds
4 eggs-beaten
Flour for dredging
 Romano cheese
Mozzarella cheese
½ tsp. mint
½ tsp. oregano
½ tsp. rosemary
Olive oil

Sauté onions and garlic in olive oil. Add 1 lg. can pureed tomatoes. Simmer on low heat for 30 minutes.

Dip eggplant in beaten eggs. Then dredge in flour.
Fry in oil for 2-3 minutes on each side. Place on paper towel to drain.

Assembly:--

Spread a little sauce on bottom of baking pan. Add one layer of eggplant. season with parsley, salt and pepper and rosemary and a thin layer of crumbled Feta cheese. Add a layer of sauce. Sprinkle with oregano , mint, Romano and Mozzarella cheeses.

Repeat layers- finish with sauce - topped off with cheese . Cover with foil. Bake @ 375deg. For 20 minutes and uncover for 15 minutes.

* use seasoned bread crumbs instead of flour as an option.

Oven Roasted Veggies

3 potatoes
2 lg. zucchini
3 large carrots
2 large summer squash
1 tbsp. parmesan cheese
2 apples- peeled
1 large eggplant
Olive oil
Salt and pepper

Slice all veggies and fruit, same size for even cooking.

Place all veggies in a lg. mixing bowl. Add olive oil to coat.
 and place them on a baking sheet.
Bake @350 deg. For about 30 minutes or until tender and a light golden
color. Put on serving platter and sprinkle with parmesan cheese.

Pan Fried Brussels Sprouts

15 Brussel sprouts -- trimmed and halved
2 tbs. butter or margarine
Salt and pepper to taste
1 tbsp. parmesan cheese
¼ tbsp. garlic salt

 Melt the butter In a non stick fry pan and add brussel sprouts. Cook on
med.-high heat. Add salt and pepper, simmer covered for 10 minutes, Stir
occasionally. Half way through cooking add garlic salt.

When done -remove from heat and add parmesan cheese. Let sit, covered
for 5 minutes.

Serves 4
* Goes well with any meat dish

Sweet Baked Squash

5 butternut squash-peeled and quartered
¼ tsp. nutmeg
¼ tsp. ground ginger
¼ tsp. ground cloves
Salt and pepper to taste
2 tbsp. brown sugar
15 caramel pieces
½ cup cream
4 tbsp. butter-melted
1 tsp. cinnamon

Brush squash generously with melted butter, salt and pepper . Bake at 350 deg. uncovered until tender.
Place squash in a bowl . Mash until chunky. Add remaining butter and mix. Add cinnamon, nutmeg, ginger, cloves, brown sugar, caramel pieces and cream.

Stir well. Taste to adjust salt. If It needs to be sweeter add more caramel and brown sugar.
Add mix to a well buttered baking pan. Cook uncovered at 350 deg. Until lightly golden brown and thickened. Allow to sit for 10 minutes before serving.

Main Courses

Main Courses

Souvlaki--------Lamb on a Skewer
Sheppard's Pie
Baked Chicken and Stuffing Casserole
Soudzoukakia----Sausages in Tomato Sauce
Stifado----Beef with Onions
Flank Steak Roll Ups
Spaghetti Stew
Stuffed Cabbage
Creamed Chipped Beef on Toast
Moussaka----Eggplant
Roast Leg of Lamb
One Dish Chicken and Stuffing
Baked Lamb Shanks
Chicken Divan
Beef in Wine Sauce
Lahanorizo-------Cabbage Rice
Pork Chop Casserole
Baked Pork Chops with Tomatoes
Easy Mac n Cheesy
One Pan Pasta Meal
Orange Marmalade Chicken
Ham and Elbow Casserole
Turkey Parmesan Casserole
Oven Crusted Chicken
Veggie Rice Stuffed Peppers---Lentil Dish
Turkey Rice Casserole
Pasta Primavera
Teriyaki Beef-Steak Sandwiches

Lemon-Butter Pasta
Broccoli and Tomato Pasta
Keftedakia---- Meatballs with Mint
Smothered Chicken and Noodles
Crispy Lemon Chicken
Meat Loaf
Herb Coated Fish Filets
Chicken Veggie Casserole
Crusty Parmesan Chicken
Meat Balls in Sauce
Big Batch Spaghetti Sauce
Pasticcio------ Baked Macaroni with Ground Beef
Creamy Spaghetti and Broccoli
Asparagus Stuffed Pork Roast
Barbecued Spare Ribs
Potato Pancakes
Brown Chicken in Yogurt Sauce
Baked Tomato Mac n Cheese
Stuffed Shells
Tomato Chicken on Rice
Stuffed Peppers and Potatoes
Pita Pockets ---The Mexican Flare
Lazy Man's Lasagna
Kapama------Spaghetti and Chicken
Kielbasa with Pineapple

Lamb on a Skewer------Souvláki

1 leg of lamb-boned and cubed
4 baby lamb kidneys
¼ cup olive oil
¼ cup lemon juice
¼ cup wine
¼ tsp. thyme
¼ tsp. oregano
¼ tsp. rosemary

1 bay leaf-crushed
2 garlic cloves-crushed
 pepper
8 bay leaves-cut
tomatoes-cut in ¼'s
green peppers-cubed
salt
oregano and lemons cut in ¼'s

**cut the lamb in small cubes--

Place the lamb and kidney cubes in a lg. bowl.
Make a marinade with the oil, lemon juice, wine, herbs, garlic and pepper.
Pour over meat. Marinate over night in fridge.
Put meat onto skewers alternating with the tomatoes, peppers and bay
leaves.
Grill the meat -brushing the pieces with the remaining marinade. Turn them
frequently to cook evenly.
Season with salt and pepper. Sprinkle crushed oregano all over meat. Serve
on the skewers or remove the pieces and serve on a platter with lemon
wedges.

***Serve with fried garlic bread or on pita bread with salad.

Sheppard's Pie

1-½ lbs. ground beef
1 lg. onion-chopped
2 tbsp. garlic salt
2 tbsp. oil
1 can mushrooms-drained and diced
6 potatoes- cooked and mashed -or 1 container ready made
1 lg. bag frozen corn-heated and drained
salt and pepper to taste
2 tbsp. Worcestershire sauce
1 tsp. cinnamon
2 tbsp. butter or margarine
2 tbsp. breadcrumbs

*****If using store bought mashed potatoes--heat in microwave for 5 minutes.**

Heat oil in pan and sauté onions. Add ground beef and cook well.
Add mushrooms and butter and cook 2 more minutes.

Lightly grease bottom of oven baking pan. (or use cooking spray)
Layer the mashed potatoes , beef mixture, and corn -ending with potatoes on top.

Sprinkle with very light layer of bread crumbs (optional)

Bake @ 350 deg. Till bubbling hot-about 25 minutes.
Crisp off under broiler till slightly brown on top. -3-4 minutes.

Allow to stand for 15 minutes before serving.

Wonderfully comforting----
****This one's for Spencie, Jay and Angela

Baked Chicken and Stuffing Casserole

4-5 lg. chicken breasts
1 lg. can cream of chicken soup
1 pkg. Swiss cheese
1 box stuffing mix--or homemade
1 can green beans-drained
pepper to taste
1 can mushrooms-drained

Place chicken in lightly greased or sprayed baking pan.
Combine the soup, cheese, mushrooms, beans, pepper and stuffing and
pour over chicken covering pieces completely.

Bake @ 350 deg. for 45-60 minutes.

****Serve with a baked potato- so good!!

Soudzoukákia ------ Sausages in Tomato Sauce

1-½ lbs. ground beef or pork
1 cup bread crumbs--moistened
2 cloves garlic-chopped
1 lg. onion-chopped
1 lg. can tomatoes
1 tsp. sugar
salt and pepper
oil

Mix together all ingredients except the oil, sugar and tomatoes.
Make rolls in the shape of sausages 4-5 inches long. Fry in hot oil-
turning them to cook on all sides.

To make the Tomato Sauce------

Mix together the tomatoes, sugar, salt and pepper.
Simmer for 15 minutes.
Add sausages to the sauce mixture. Cook for another 10 minutes
on low heat.

Stifado--------Beef with Onions

Recipe can also be used with pork.

1-½ lbs. beef
3 tbsp. butter or margarine
3 tbsp. oil
1 lg. can tomatoes-diced
¼ cup red wine vinegar
salt and pepper to taste
3 tbsp. tomato paste

2-3 bay leaves
2-3 garlic cloves-chopped
1 pkg. frozen- tiny peas
 onions--chopped -- (enough
 to double the weight of the
  meat.)---

Cut the meat into 1-inch pieces and simmer in sauce pan with butter and oil.
Add tomatoes, peas, vinegar, salt, pepper, and tomato paste.
Mix well.
Then add cloves, garlic, bay leaves and onions. Stir well.

Add enough water to half cover the contents of the saucepan.

Cover and simmer for about 1-½ hours until meat is tender and liquid is reduced to a gravy.

******Serves 8
****Can also be cooked in a crock pot.--

Flank Steak Roll Ups

2 lbs. beef flank steak-- (I often use cube steak)
¼ cup butter or margarine
1 lg. onion-finely chopped
½ cup celery-finely chopped
2 cups bread crumbs- dried- or bread cubes, crushed
salt and pepper to taste
½ tsp. poultry seasoning
1 cup beef broth
2 tsp. Worcestershire sauce

Cut flank steak (or cube steak) in half crosswise. Score on both sides
by slashing lightly in a criss- cross pattern. ---set aside.

Saute butter, onion and celery till onions are transparent.
Add bread crumbs , salt and pepper, and poultry seasoning.
Toss lightly.

Spread half of stuffing across the center on each piece of steak.
Fold the sides over stuffing. Secure with string or tooth picks.

Place rolls in 8x8 baking dish-seam side down. Mix together broth and
Worcestershire sauce . Pour over steak pieces.

Cook in microwave - cover with plastic wrap-for 30-35 minutes --or in oven
@350.deg. For 1-½ hours till fork tender.- (12 minutes per lb.) Turn rolls
every 15 minutes.

Let stand for 10 minutes uncovered.

Spaghetti Stew

1-½ lbs. stew beef-cubed
flour
salt and pepper
1 lg. onion-chopped
4 cups water
3 carrots-sliced
2 celery stalks-sliced
4 oz. spaghetti-cut in 2 inch lengths
1 can peas
3 tbsp. butter or margarine

Season the beef cubes with salt and pepper. Roll in flour-cover each piece well.
Brown the meat in butter or margarine. (can use oil) Add onions and water- cover and simmer for 2 hours.

Add remaining ingredients. Simmer till done-about 30 minutes.
***Add more liquid if needed.

****Serves 6

Stuffed Cabbage

1 medium head of cabbage
1 lg. onion-minced
1 lb. ground beef
salt and pepper to taste
3 tbsp. ketchup
¼ tsp. Worcestershire sauce
1 cup rice

Cook rice as directed. ---set aside

Cook whole cabbage in boiling, salted water and drain. Remove core and separate the cabbage leaves.

Sauté onions till brown. Add ground beef and cook completely.
Add salt, pepper, rice, ketchup, and Worcestershire sauce .Mix well.
Stuff center of each cabbage leave with mixture and fold them like an envelope.

Place in greased baking dish. Add tomato sauce and water.
½ and ½ amounts-Cover and bake @350 deg. for about 30 -45 minutes.

Serve with a salad, Greek bread--- a meal fit for a king!

Creamed Chipped Beef on Toast

1-½ lbs. chipped beef
3 tbsp. butter
2 tbsp. flour
2 cups milk
¾ cups grated cheese
salt and pepper to taste

Cut meat in very small pieces.
Place in saucepan-add water just enough to cover the meat. Cover and simmer to cook meat -and drain

Brown the beef in a pan with butter.
Add flour, milk, salt, and pepper.

**To make a thick sauce- simmer long enough to cook the flour.
    For thinner sauce-add a little beef stock or water.

**Serve on toast or baked potatoes and sprinkle with parmesan cheese.

Moussaká------Eggplant

1 lb. ground beef
3 tbsp. butter
1 lg. onion-chopped
1 cup tomato sauce
¾ cup dried bread crumbs
1 cup grated cheese
3 tbsp. parsley-chopped
1 cup (drinking) white wine
1 cup water
4 medium size eggplants
salt and pepper to taste
butter- melted

***To prepare white sauce (Béchamel) --
In a saucepan---
Add 1 cup flour to 1 quart milk. Blend well. Mix in 4 tbsp. butter, 2 eggs,
salt and pepper to taste.-----

Sauté onions in butter. Add ground beef and chop it up in the pan.
Cook until mixture is crumbly. Add tomato sauce, wine, water, salt, pepper
And parsley.
Cover--cook on low heat for 1 hour.

   ***While this is cooking, slice the egg plant in ¼ inch thick pieces.
Sprinkle them with salt on both sides and allow them to sit in a colander
to extract the water.--Deep fry the eggplant slices in hot oil.

**Prepare the white sauce at this time-----
Arrange the eggplant slices in a shallow pan. (don't over lap them)
Sprinkle some of the bread crumbs on top . Add the chopped meat evenly
over pan. Sprinkle ½ the grated cheese and ½ the bread crumbs over meat.
Pour the white sauce over entire top. and sprinkle remaining cheese and
crumbs.
Pour melted butter over top. Bake @350.deg. For 15 minutes until golden
brown.

**Allow to cool before cutting into square pieces.--This one's for keeps!

Roast Leg of Lamb

Spring lamb is tender and cooks well.

leg of lamb
garlic cloves -several- peeled
olive oil
juice of 1 lemon
salt and pepper to taste
1 tbsp. oregano

Make slits all along top of lamb with a pointed knife. Fill each opening
with garlic cloves.

***Marinating mixture--
Combine oil, salt, pepper, oregano and lemon juice. Mix well.
Rub mixture all over the lamb -both sides.

Cover and marinate in fridge over night.

Brush bottom of pan with oil. Place lamb in center of pan.
Cover and bake @ 350 deg.
If lamb is over 3 lbs. --cook for about 2 hours.

Baste meat with pan drippings every 20 minutes or so. Uncover towards
The end and continue to cook till meat is brown on top.

***Allow to sit for 15-20 minutes before slicing.

****Serve with rice and salad!

*****It doesn't get any better!

One Dish Chicken and Stuffing Bake

4 cups herb stuffing mix
4-6 skinless- boneless chicken breasts
½ tsp. paprika
2 cans (10-¾) oz. cream of celery soup
1 tbsp. fresh parsley-chopped
1-¼ water-boiling
4 tbsp. margarine
2/3 cup milk

Mix stuffing, boiling water and margarine together.
Spoon stuffing mixture across the center of a 3 or 4 quart-shallow
baking dish.
Place the chicken around the stuffing and sprinkle paprika over the
 chicken.

Mix the soup, milk and parsley. Pour over the chicken.

Bake- covered with foil @ 400 deg. For 30 minutes or until desired
doneness.

****Use a 3 qt. dish for 4 chicken breasts.
   ***and 4 qt. dish for 6 chicken breasts.

****Really Good-----

Baked Lamb Shanks

4-6 lamb shanks
salt and pepper
2 cloves garlic-minced
2 carrots-cut in strips
1 lg. onion - sliced
2 stalks celery-cut in strips
1 bay leaf
1 tsp. oregano
½ tsp. thyme
1 (8 0z) can tomato sauce
1 cup water
¼ cup olive oil   * * *   Pre-heat oven to 375 deg.

Sprinkle lamb shanks with salt and pepper to taste- and rub with garlic.
Scatter the chopped veggies in the bottom of the roasting pan large
enough to hold the lamb. Put the shanks on top of the veggies and
Sprinkle them with oregano and thyme

Combine the tomato sauce and water and add it to the pan.
Drizzle olive oil over all.
Cover tightly with a lid and bake for 2 hours.

Meat should be browned, the sauce will be reduced and the meat tender.

Skim off the excess fat.

****The meat will be so tender it will be falling off the bone.
*** Amazing dish!!

**Serves 4-6

Chicken Divan

2 cups chicken pieces-cooked
1 pkg. frozen broccoli cuts
1 lg. can cream of mushroom soup
salt and pepper
1 lg. onion-chopped
1 tsp. oil
1 tbsp. butter
bread crumbs
grated cheese

Sauté the onions in oil in a deep pan till tender.
 Add chicken pieces with broccoli cuts and stir.
Blend in the butter.

Add cream of mushroom soup, salt and pepper and
mix well.
Pour the mixture over the chicken covering each piece
completely.

Top off with bread crumbs and grated cheese.
Bake for 30 minutes.

****A perfect dish any time.***

Beef in Wine Sauce

2 lbs. stew beef
1 small can mushrooms
1 small can mushroom soup
1 tsp. garlic powder
salt and pepper to taste
½ cup dry wine (good for drinking)
1/3 cup water
½ pkg. onion soup

Sprinkle meat with garlic salt, salt and pepper- covering meat thoroughly.

Mix all ingredients in a casserole dish.
Bake @ 325 deg. for about 3 hours.

***Serve with any pasta noodles and a good crusty bread.

Lahanorizo ---- Cabbage Rice

1 medium cabbage-- cut and sliced
1 cup rice
1 tbsp. olive oil
1 onion--sliced
3 fresh tomatoes-mashed (can tomatoes can be used)
juice of one lemon
salt and pepper

Wash the cabbage and cut into slices.

In a sauce pan -sauté the onions in oil. Add the cabbage and stir.
Add 2 cups water, tomatoes, and mix well. Cook for 10 minutes
and then add the rice. Stir well.

Cook for about 20 minutes or until rice is done. Add salt and
pepper to taste.
Add a few drops of lemon juice into individual bowls.

****Serve hot or cold

Pork Chop Casserole

4 -thick boneless pork chops
2 cups long grain rice-uncooked
1 lg. onion-chopped
¼ tsp. basil-chopped
1 stick butter or margarine
2 cans beef broth
1 cup water
1 pkg. mushrooms
1 pkg. frozen peas
salt and pepper

Pre-heat oven @ 350 deg.--

Place chops in a 2 quart baking dish.
Spread the rice, mushrooms, onions, and peas around the chops. Add salt, pepper, and basil.

Cover with broth and water.
Spread margarine or butter, in pieces, equally over mixture.

Bake, covered-for 1 hour. Stir only occasionally. Add more water or broth if needed.

*****Melts in your mouth!
    *****Try a green salad on the side.

Baked Pork Chops with Tomato

4-6 center cut pork chops
1 lg. onion-chopped
1 lg. can tomato sauce
2 cups water
2 carrots-sliced
2 celery stalks-diced
salt and pepper
1 tbsp. garlic salt
1 tbsp. oregano
2 tbsp. Worcestershire sauce

Place chops in lg. baking pan.

Combine onions, celery, carrots, salt and pepper,
garlic powder, oregano, tomato sauce, water and Worcestershire
sauce. Pour over chops.

Bake @ 350 deg.-uncovered for about 1 hour.

***Serve on a bed of rice and cranberry sauce.

Easy Mac n Cheesy

1 stick butter or margarine - melted
3-4 tbsp. flour
salt and pepper
2 cups milk-cold
1 box macaroni--cooked and drained
1 bag shredded cheddar cheese (save a little for topping)
bread crumbs

Melt the butter and add enough flour to thicken. Stir well.
Add cold milk and whisk to a boil. Add salt and pepper
and shredded cheese. Mix well.

Add macaroni -stir and put into casserole dish. Bake @ 350 deg.
For 25 minutes.
Then add bread crumbs on top and more cheese. Put under broiler for a
minute or 2 just to melt the cheese.

***Grandkids love it! Great at a cook out!

One Pan Pasta Meal

1 lg. onion- diced
1 lb. ground beef
2-½ cups water
1 lg. green pepper- diced
1 can mushrooms
3-½ cups pasta (rigatoni or penne)
1 lg. jar spaghetti sauce -(your choice)
1 pkg. shredded mozzarella cheese -divided
1 cup grated parmesan cheese
½ tsp. cinnamon
2 tbsp. oil
salt and pepper to taste

In a lg. skillet--
Sauté onion, peppers, and mushrooms in oil till tender.
Add meat till brown and cooked thoroughly . Add cinnamon, salt and pepper. Add water -bring to a boil.

Add pasta. At the boiling point, reduce heat, stir and simmer for 15 minutes or until pasta is done.

Stir in spaghetti sauce and 1 cup of mozzarella cheese.
Top off with left over cheeses .

Cover and cook on low heat for a few more minutes for cheese to melt.

**** So Easy . --Serve with mixed vegetables!

Orange Marmalade Chicken

1 cup brown sugar-packed
6-8 chicken pieces (your choice)
2 cups orange juice
¾ cup orange marmalade
salt and pepper to taste

Combine the orange juice, marmalade and brown sugar.
Mix till completely incorporated. Season with salt and pepper.

Place chicken pieces in a well greased cooking pan. Pour mixture over
chicken coating them well.

Allow to marinate in fridge for 2 hours, turning chicken every ½ hour

Cover and bake @ 350 deg. For 1 hour .
Uncover and finish cooking for another 1-½ hours or until fully cooked.

Let stand for 15 minutes before serving.

******Works well with a baked potato and veggie
     *** Add Greek bread and your meal is complete.

Ham and Elbow Casserole

2 cups elbow macaroni
2 cups cooked baked ham-cubed
1 lg. can cream of mushroom soup
1 -8 oz. container plain yogurt
1 cup carrots--shredded
1 medium onion- finely chopped
1 small green pepper- finely chopped
½ tbsp. Italian seasoning
½ cup buttered bread crumbs

Cook macaroni as directed and drain.
Combine all ingredients -except- bread crumbs. Mix well!

Pour into a 2-½ quart casserole pan.
Sprinkle bread crumbs on top.
      Bake @ 350 deg. For 30 minutes till bubbly.

****Serves 4-6

Turkey Parmesan Casserole

8 oz. spaghetti-broken in half, cooked and drained
2 cups cooked turkey-chopped
1 can cream of mushroom soup (10-¾ oz.)
3 cups frozen broccoli flowerets-thawed (or fresh)
1 cup sour cream
1 cup grated parmesan cheese- divided

In a lg. bowl mix all the ingredient except ¼ cup of the parmesan cheese. Pour mixture into a 2 quart casserole dish and sprinkle the remaining parmesan cheese over top.

Bake @ 350 deg. For about 25-30 minutes or until thoroughly heated.

**** Makes 4-6 servings

***A great one dish meal!

Oven Crusted Chicken

1 stick butter or margarine -melted
1/3 cup all purpose flour
1-½ tsp salt
1/8 tsp. thyme
1/8 tsp. crushed rosemary
1/8 tsp. marjoram
1-½ cups corn flakes- crushed
3 lbs. chicken pieces--skin removed

Pre-heat oven @ 375 deg.

In a lg. bowl- Combine melted butter, flour, salt, thyme, rosemary, and marjoram.

Put cereal in a separate dish.

Dip chicken in butter sauce mixture . Roll chicken in cereal till well coated. Place pieces in a baking pan.

Bake @350 deg. for about 1 hour to 1 hour and 15 minutes. Make sure chicken is thoroughly cooked and golden brown.

***Serves 6--
***Keeps well in the fridge

Veggie Rice Stuffed Peppers--Lentil Dish

1 lg. zucchini --cut into small pieces
1 cup onions- minced
1 cup rice--cooked
1 cup grated cheddar cheese
4 green peppers
1 tbsp. olive oil
salt and pepper to taste
½ tsp. garlic salt

Cook rice as directed.

Sauté zucchini and onions in olive oil till tender.
Mix zucchini, onions, rice, garlic salt, salt and pepper and grated cheese together.

Wash peppers, cut off caps and remove seeds.
Stuff peppers with mixture . Add more grated cheese on top
of each pepper.

Bake @ 350 deg. For about 1 hour -till peppers are tender and hot.

***Cooking peppers in water prior to stuffing helps the cooking
 Process--(optional)

***Serve with a Greek salad!

Turkey Rice Casserole

1 lg. onion-chopped
1 cup mayonnaise
1 can cream of celery soup
1 can green beans or French beans
turkey-or chicken chunks-- cooked
1-½ cups rice - cooked

Cook rice as directed.

Sauté onions and mix with cooked rice. Add mayonnaise, cream of celery soup, and beans. Mix well.

Add chicken. (or turkey)
Bake @ 375 deg. till hot and bubbly.

******Tastes amazing !
Great for leftovers served on toast

Pasta Primavera

1-8 0z. Pkg. cream cheese
1/2 stick butter or margarine
1 cup grated parmesan cheese
½ cup milk -or ½ and ½
1 box fettuccini

1 small can of each of the following-- (or frozen)

Peas or corn, cut green beans, carrots, sliced yellow or red pepper, broccoli and asparagus. (cut up)--you may substitute--

Cook pasta as directed, drain and set aside.

While cooking pasta-steam all veggies for about 4 minutes. (a few minutes longer if frozen)
 Don't want them to be soggy..

In lg. sauce pan stir together the cream cheese, parmesan cheese, butter and milk (or cream)-on medium heat. Stir constantly till smooth.

Add cooked veggies and simmer a few minutes longer.
Toss cream cheese mixture and pasta together and sprinkle parmesan cheese on top.

****Great family feast!

Teriyaki Beef- Steak Sandwiches

3 lbs. roast beef
¼ cup oil
½ cup soy sauce
2 tbsp. molasses
pepper to taste
2 tsp. ground ginger
2 tbsp. honey
2 tsp. mustard

Mix all ingredients and place in lg. plastic bag with the meat.
Shake well to cover all he meat.
Marinate for 1 hour in fridge.

Put a layer of meat in pan and broil both sides. (one layer at a time)
Until all the meat is cooked. --approximately 1 minute on each side.

****Put in sub rolls, pita pockets or favorite bread along with your favorite
accompaniments such as lettuce, tomatoes, pickles, mushrooms, onions,
 peppers and cucumbers.

   ***Serve with Cole slaw

Lemon -Butter Pasta

1 box linguini
3/4 stick butter or margarine
¼ cup lemon juice
¼ tsp. garlic-crushed
½ tsp. parsley-chopped

Cook pasta as directed and drain. (save ½ cup of pasta water)
Place pasta back in pot.
Add butter, lemon juice crushed garlic, and parsley. Mix well.

****So simple and abundantly delicious!!

Broccoli and Tomato Pasta

1 small onion- finely chopped
1 tbsp. olive oil
2 lg. cans tomatoes- diced   1 tsp. tomato paste
1 tsp. garlic-minced   1 can stewed tomatoes
1 tbsp. balsamic vinegar   salt and pepper
1 tsp. basil- dried
1 box Rigatoni
1 lb. broccoli florets
1 cup Feta cheese-crumbled

Cook pasta as directed and drain and set aside.
Blanche broccoli, drain and set aside.

In pan- heat the oil on medium heat. Add garlic and onion and cook till
tender. Add tomatoes with liquid, vinegar, basil, onions, tomato paste, and
stewed tomatoes. Season with salt and pepper to taste.

Simmer for about 15-18 minutes-stirring often.
Add all ingredients to the pasta in a family size bowl. Crumble Feta cheese
on top and drizzle olive oil all over pasta.

*****SERVES 4

Keftedákia-------- Meatballs with Mint

1 cup fresh white bread crumbs
¼ cup Ouzo--water or wine may be substituted
6 tbsp. olive oil
1 lg. onion - grated
1 lb. ground beef- or lamb
1 egg
1 tbsp. fresh mint-chopped
1 clove garlic-minced
½ tsp. oregano- chopped
salt and pepper to taste
flour

Soak the bread crumbs in Ouzo . (wine or water)
Sauté the onions in oil until translucent, drain and place in a deep bowl.
Squeeze out the bread crumbs.

Mix the bread crumbs, onions, beef, egg, mint, garlic, oregano, salt and
pepper till well incorporated. (hands are your best tools)

Form into 1 inch balls, roll them in the flour, and refrigerate for 2 hours.

Pre-heat the oil in the skillet , adding more if necessary during the cooking.
(needs to be very hot)

Fry meatballs in batches--not crowding them in the pan. Turn them
frequently.--Cook until crispy and brown.

Remove and drain on paper towels.

***Serve hot or chilled with a yogurt and chopped chives dip.
   ***Wonderful with pasta and salad..

Smothered Chicken and Noodles

chicken pieces--cut up same size
½ cup flour
½ cup milk
1 medium onion- chopped
1 small can mushrooms-chopped
1 shallot- diced
1 can cream of mushroom soup
1 box egg noodles
2 tbsp. butter or margarine
Feta cheese

Cover chicken pieces thoroughly with flour. Shake off excess.

Fry in hot oil till crispy and brown on all sides. Remove chicken and place on paper towel.

In separate fry pan add butter and sauté onions, mushrooms, and shallots till tender.
Add chicken pieces, 1 can cream of mushroom soup and milk.
Mix well.

Simmer to reduce to a thick sauce.

Cook noodles as directed and drain. Add to chicken and sauce mixture.
Serve on a platter.
Sprinkle chunks of Feta cheese all over top.

******If mixture is too thick- add a little more milk.

*****great-family style dinner. Serve with Italian bread

Crispy Lemon Chicken

½ cup vegetable oil
2 tbsp, lemon juice
parmesan cheese
chicken pieces-thinly sliced
flour
2 eggs -beaten (add 2 tbsp. water)
1 cup butter or margarine

Mix flour with the cheese.

Dip chicken in eggs- then dredge in the flour and cheese. Shake off the excess. Fry in hot oil till crispy and tender.

Remove and place on paper towels to drain. Arrange chicken on a platter. Mix lemon juice with butter and pour over chicken.

******Serve with rice, noodles or mashed potatoes!
      Sweet potatoes would be a nice accompaniment.

Meat Loaf

1 can mushrooms-drained and chopped
1-½ lbs. ground beef
½ lb. pork
1 lg. onion- diced
½ can diced tomatoes-drained
2 tbsp. parsley- chopped
5 tbsp. ketchup
salt and pepper
I tbsp. Worcestershire sauce
4 slices of thick bread- soaked in milk and squeezed
2 eggs-slightly beaten

Place all ingredients in a lg. bowl. Mix well with your hands till well incorporated.
Place onto a greased cooking sheet and shape into a loaf.

Bake @ 350 deg. for about 1 hour to 1 hour and 20 minutes till golden brown and crusty on top.

Herb Coated Fish Filets

½ cup corn meal
½ tsp. paprika
salt and pepper to taste
1-½ lbs. fresh or frozen fish filets-thawed
2 eggs-beaten
2 tbsp. milk
2 tbsp. margarine-melted
lemon

Pre-heat oven to 350 deg.--

Combine corn meal and seasonings. Dip fish in combined milk and eggs.
Coat fish with corn meal mixture. Place on lightly greased sheet pan.
Pour margarine over fish.

Bake for about 20 minutes till crispy and golden brown.
Squeeze lemon over top while fish is warm.

******Serve on a bed of rice!

Chicken Veggie Casserole

¼ cup margarine
¼ cup all purpose flour
1 lg. can peas-drained
1 lg. can carrots- drained
1 lg. can chicken broth
1-14 ½ oz. can evaporated milk
2 cups water
1 can chicken gravy
2-½ cups chicken-cooked and diced
2 cups rice-cooked
1 small can mushrooms-drained and diced

Melt margarine and blend in flour. Add broth, milk, and water. Mix well.

Cook on low heat-stirring constantly till thick. Add salt and pepper, chicken, veggies and cooked rice. Pour into a greased baking dish.

Bake @ 350. Deg. For about 30 minutes till bubbly and hot.

*****Serve with garden salad!

Crusty Parmesan Chicken

1-½ cups bread crumbs
1/2 cup grated parmesan cheese
1 tsp. garlic powder
salt and pepper
1 stick butter or margarine-melted
3 lbs. chicken pieces
1 tsp. parsley-chopped
½ tsp. paprika

To make crumb mixture---
Combine bread crumbs, parmesan cheese, paprika, garlic powder,
salt and pepper and parsley.

Dip chicken into melted butter and roll in bread crumb mixture.
Place chicken- skin side up on greased baking pan.

Bake @ 350 deg. For about 1 hour.

****Chicken should be golden brown and crispy!

Meat Balls in Sauce

3 lbs. hamburg
salt and pepper   Sauce--
3 eggs
2 medium onions- chopped   1 lg. can tomatoes
1 green pepper-chopped   1 can tomato paste
3 cloves garlic- minced   salt and pepper
1 tsp. parsley   1 clove garlic-minced
½ tsp. crushed red pepper seeds   1 bay leaf
4 drops tabasco sauce   1 lg. can   tomato sauce
6 slices bread-soaked in milk and squeezed

In a lg. bowl add hamburg, eggs, onion, green pepper, garlic , red pepper
seeds, parsley, tabasco sauce , bread and salt and pepper.
Mix well till all ingredients are well incorporated.

Add I tsp. olive oil to a non-stick hot fry pan. Brown the meatballs in small
batches till golden brown on all sides. Drain some of the oil.

      In a lg. pot--
 Add tomatoes, tomato paste, salt and pepper, garlic, bay leaf, and tomato
sauce. Simmer on low heat for ½ hour. Than add cooked
meatballs to sauce and simmer on low heat another 15 minutes.
Remove bay leaf.

*****Can be used over pasta, in a sandwich or as an appetizer.

      ****for extra thick sauce-add more tomato paste---

Big Batch Spaghetti Sauce

Olive oil
1-½ lb. ground beef
1 lg. carrot finely chopped
1 medium green pepper-chopped
1 lg. onion- chopped
1 tbsp. Worcestershire sauce
1 tsp. cinnamon
salt and pepper to taste
1 tsp. garlic salt

1/2 tsp. garlic powder
½ tsp. onion powder
1 small can mushrooms-diced
1 lg. can diced tomatoes
  (with liquid)
1 lg. can crushed tomatoes
2 tbsp. margarine

In a lg. pot---

Sauté onions, mushrooms, peppers and carrots in a little oil-till tender.
Add ground beef and cook well.
Season with cinnamon, onion powder, garlic salt, Worcestershire sauce, and salt and pepper. Stir well.

Add diced tomatoes with liquid and crushed tomatoes. Stir well and simmer uncovered- on low heat for about 35-40 minutes. Stir occasionally.

Add margarine and cook another 5 minutes.
   Sprinkle with parmesan cheese and chopped scallions

****Serve over your favorite pasta or add pasta into the sauce and serve on a platter.
    ***   Recipe can be cut in half and freezes well.

Pasticcio---Baked Macaroni with Ground Beef

1-½ lbs. macaroni

To make Meat Sauce-- ---

1 lb. ground beef	1 tsp. cinnamon
1 stick butter	½ tsp. allspice
1 lg. onion-chopped	1 garlic clove-minced
1 lg. can tomato sauce	bread crumbs
salt and pepper to taste	

Sauté ground beef In a little butter and add all above ingredients till well cooked.

To make White Sauce----

4 cups milk-hot   --- ¼ tsp. grated nutmeg
3eggs --separate yolks and whites
½ cup butter
1 cup grated parmesan cheese (or Kefalotiri cheese)
1 cup flour
salt and pepper

Cook macaroni-drain, add ½ the butter and set aside.
Prepare the meat sauce as directed in the recipe.

Then add 3 unbeaten egg whites and ½ the cheese to the macaroni and mix well.
Butter the baking pan and sprinkle bottom with dried bread crumbs.-Add macaroni. Add ½ dried bread crumbs to meat sauce and spread over top.
Cover with white sauce to which 3 unbeaten egg yolks, part of the cheese, and nutmeg have been added.
Sprinkle with remaining grated cheese and more bread crumbs- to form a crust.
Pour over the remaining warm butter.

Bake @ 350 deg. Till golden brown… Allow to cool before cutting..

Creamy Spaghetti and Broccoli

1 lg. onion-chopped
1 lb. spaghetti-cooked and drained--set aside
1 lg. can cream of mushroom soup
1 pkg. frozen broccoli florets-blanched for 4 minutes
2 tbsp. parsley-chopped
1 cup heavy cream
½ cup milk
salt and pepper to taste
grated cheese (your favorite)
2 tbsp. butter or margarine

Sauté onions in oil till tender.
Add cream and milk to cream of mushroom soup . Heat and stir
thoroughly. Add cooked onions, salt, pepper, butter and broccoli. Cook for
a minute or two more.

Add spaghetti to mixture and stir well. Add parsley last few minutes.
Sprinkle grated cheese over top.

****If sauce is too thick add a little more milk!

*******Serve with garlic bread and favorite wine!

Asparagus Stuffed Pork Roast

1 pork roast--6-8 lbs
1 lg. onion-chopped
½ tsp. sage
asparagus-small bunch-trim off ends
½ tsp. coriander
salt and pepper
1 lemon- thinly sliced
½ cup celery-diced
½ tsp. garlic salt
½ tsp. onion powder
olive oil
Butchers string

Sauté onions, garlic and celery in a little oil till tender.
Season with salt and pepper.-Take off heat to cool.

Filet the roast as you would a jelly roll to open it up.
Salt and pepper the entire inside. Sprinkle with sage, coriander,
garlic salt and onion powder. Spread the cooled onion mixture over
the inside of the meat. Layer the asparagus so that the pieces are showing at
both ends.

Roll the roast into a log shape and tie it with butcher's string at 2-3 inch
Intervals- to hold it's shape. Rub meat with olive oil and sprinkle with
salt, pepper and garlic salt.

Place in lightly greased , shallow roasting pan.
Arrange lemon slices along top of meat.

Bake at 325 to 350 deg. for 1 hour or till done.

*****Serve with potato and salad!

Barbecued Spare Ribs

8-10 spare ribs-or more
1 cup teriyaki sauce
½ cup maple syrup
salt and pepper to taste
1 lg. onion -thinly sliced

In lg. bowl mix teriyaki sauce , maple syrup and salt and pepper.
Brush the mixture generously over the ribs on both sides.

Place ribs in roasting pan with onions .
Bake @ 350 deg. For about 1 hour basting ribs half way through
till done.

****Serve with rice or noodles and corn on the cob!-mmm

Potato Pancakes

vegetable oil
1 lb. (3 cups) shredded potatoes
½ cup onion-chopped
½ cup pancake or waffle mix
2 tbsp. water

Use a lg. skillet--

Heat oil- ¼ inch deep -on medium heat to 375 deg..
 Combine all ingredients and mix well.

Drop ¼ cup mixture onto skillet- shaping into a circle. Fry for 2-3
minutes on each side-until golden brown. Continue process until done.

*****Serve with fruit, jam or applesauce

Brown Chicken in Yogurt Sauce

4-6 chicken pieces
1 cup flour
1 lg. onion-chopped
¾ cup plain yogurt
½ cup white wine
1 tbsp. oil

Flour the chicken-(shake off the excess).
Add oil to hot skillet and brown the chicken on both sides. Add onion and brown.
Add wine and lower heat. Cook for about 30 minutes.

Stir in yogurt and cook a few minutes longer.
Mixture should be a little thick.

****** Serve with rice---YUM!-

Baked Tomato Mac"n"Cheese

1 lg. can crushed tomatoes-with liquid
1 lg. onion-chopped
salt and pepper
1 lb. ziti
1 pkg. shredded cheddar cheese
6 tbsp. butter or margarine
1 tbsp. oil

Cook pasta as directed. Pre-heat oven @ 350 deg.

Sauté onions in butter and oil until golden brown.
Add tomatoes (with liquid) . Cook another 2 minutes. Add salt and pepper.
Drain pasta- combine with mixture. Place in greased casserole dish Mix in
cheddar cheese.

Bake uncovered in pre-heated oven @ 350 deg. For about 45 minutes.

*******A wonderful cook out dish as well as a main meal

Stuffed Shells

Shells--cook and set aside
1 lg. onion-chopped
1-½ lb. Hamburg
2 pkgs. frozen spinach-thawed and drained
1 pkg. cream cheese-softened
1 cup cottage cheese
1 cup cheddar cheese
1 lg. can tomatoes- diced
1 lg. can tomato sauce
1 pkg. mozzarella cheese
 Pepper to taste
½ tsp. garlic salt

Sauté Hamburg and onions and allow to cool. Drain some of liquid.
Mix in drained spinach, cottage cheese, cream cheese, pepper
and garlic salt.

Stuff the cooked shells with Hamburg mixture and place in baking pan..
Cover with tomatoes and sauce .
Then top with cheddar cheese and mozzarella cheese.

Cover and bake @ 350 deg. For 1 hour.

****Comfort food--delicious!

Tomato Chicken on Rice

6 chicken thighs
2 cups tomato sauce
salt and pepper to taste
¾ tsp. oregano
1-½ cups rice--long grain
½ tsp. garlic salt
1 lg onion-diced
4 carrots- cut in rounds
½ cup olive oil
2 cups water
1 small can peas

Cook rice as directed. Set aside.

In a glass oven pan - add tomato sauce, salt, pepper, oregano, garlic salt, onion, carrots, peas and oil. Mix well.

Place chicken pieces in pan and add water.
Cover and cook @ 350 deg. For 1-½ hours. Add more water if necessary while cooking.
Uncover and continue cooking till chicken is done.

********Serve over rice and a vegetable.

Stuffed Peppers and Potatoes

6-8 medium peppers - cut off tops-wash and remove seeds
1-½ lbs. ground beef
1 cup rice--uncooked
1 lg. onion-finely chopped
2 tbsp. oil
1 tbsp. tomato paste
salt and pepper to taste
½ tsp. oregano
1 egg-well beaten
4-8 oz. cans tomato sauce
3 cups water
6 lg. potatoes-peeled and quartered
½ tsp. garlic powder

Boil peppers in water for about 5 minutes to tenderize. Drain and dry.
Combine remaining ingredients except tomato sauce and water.

Fill peppers with mixture. Place peppers on their side in a deep roasting pan
in a circle. Turn peppers every 15 minutes while cooking.

Combine remaining tomato paste, tomato sauce and water.
Mix and pour over peppers.

Place potatoes in center of pan.
 Bake @ 400 deg. for 1 hour and 15 minutes
till rice is done.

*** Fabulous!! Serve with a salad and bread rolls

Pita Pockets-----The Mexican Flare

½ lb. ground beef
1 lg. onion -chopped
1-16 oz. can pork and beans
1 cup salsa
pita pockets
2 cups shredded lettuce
1-½ cups tomatoes-chopped
1 cup shredded cheddar cheese
1 container plain yogurt
1 container sour cream

Mix sour cream and yogurt together.
Sauté ground beef with onions and drain liquid. Add beans and salsa
And heat through.

Assemble pockets with mixture and add lettuce, tomatoes, cheese, yogurt
and sour cream.

***********Great party favorite !!

Lazy Man's Lasagna

2-lb. container ricotta cheese
1 lb. lg. macaroni
3 eggs
½ tsp. parsley-chopped
pepper to taste
½ cup parmesan cheese
1 lg. jar pasta sauce (or homemade)

Cook macaroni as directed and drain.- set aside.

In a bowl---

Mix ricotta cheese, eggs, pepper, parsley, and 2 tbsp. grated cheese
Mix macaroni with ricotta mixture and cheese.

Use a deep baking dish and bake @ 350 deg. For about 45 minutes.

Kapamá-----Spaghetti and Chicken

1 pkg. spaghetti
4 chicken breasts
olive oil
2 lg. onions-chopped
2 cloves garlic-sliced or minced
½ tsp. cinnamon
salt and pepper to taste
juice of 1 lemon
1 lg. can tomato sauce
cloves-(to taste)
water

Brown the chicken in one tsp. oil. Add onions, and garlic and saute till onions are transparent.

Season with salt and pepper. Add the cinnamon, cloves and lemon juice . Stir well. Cook for about 5 minutes.

Add tomato sauce and about ½ cup water and cook for 1-½ hours on medium to low heat.

Add more water , if needed , during the cooking. Sauce should remain thick.

Cook spaghetti as directed.
Place pasta on individual dishes or on a lg. serving platter and arrange chicken on top. Pour the sauce over the dish.

****Add cheese to your liking--and enjoy! Wine is great with this dish..

Kielbasa with Pineapple

2 kielbasa sausage rings
½ jar currants
1-lg. can pineapples -crushed

Boil kielbasa (whole).
Drain and slice. Heat pineapple and currants. Pour over sausage.

***Serve hot!   Great with mashed potatoes and salad.

Fish Dishes

Fish Dishes

Stuffing for Baked Shrimp, lobster and Fish
Baked Pollock with Spinach
Baked Salmon with Dill
Tuna Salad with Curry
Baked Stuffed Scallops
Baked Shrimp
Seafood Quiche
Tuna Casserole
Shrimp Scampi and Spinach Fettuccini
Fish and Veggies cooked in foil
Greek Style Fish
Kalamarakia----Greek Squid
Simple Fish Batter
Garides Tourkolimano----Greek Shrimp
Shrimp pilaf
Shrimp Jambalaya
Fish with a Sweet Touch
Fish and Shrimp Bake

Stuffing for Baked, stuffed Shrimp, Lobster and Fish

1 pkg. graham crackers
¼ cup brown sugar
1 pkg. Ritz crackers
1 tbsp. Worcestershire sauce
Salt and pepper
½ cup melted butter (or more if desired)

Crush Ritz and Graham crackers. Place in bowl.
Add Worcestershire sauce and brown sugar. Add melted butter and mix until
well incorporated. Add salt and pepper to taste.
Put a thick layer on top of your favorite food.
Bake at 350 deg. Till done.

Baked Pollock with Spinach

¾ lb. fresh spinach
4 tbsp. margarine
1 tbsp. lemon juce
½ tsp. salt
¼ tsp pepper
½ tsp. nutmeg
1-¼ lbs. Pollock fillets
1/cup white wine
3 tbsp. grated parmesan cheese

Wash spinach- remove stems and chop.
Steam in saucepan with only the water on the leaves, until wilted. Drain and pat dry with paper towel.
Melt margarine. Add lemon juice, salt and pepper and nutmeg.
Toss with spinach.
Place fish in baking dish , add wine. Bake in pre-heated 400 deg. Oven for 10 minutes.
Spread spinach over fish. Sprinkle with cheese . Cook until fish flakes 5-10 minutes longer.

* Low sodium tip --
Use unsalted margarine, omit salt,add 3 tbsp. fresh, chopped parsley to spinach.

Baked Salmon with Dill

Salmon-1 lb. per person
Lemon juice
Fresh dill-chopped
Extra virgin olive oil
Lemon slices
1-lg. onion- sliced paper thin
Salt and pepper

Place salmon on tin foil. Rub each piece generously with oil. Sprinkle with dill, salt and pepper.
Top with alternating lemon and onion slices.
Squeeze lemon over all. Add a sprig of dill on top.
Wrap in the foil, pinching the ends to make a tight seal.
Bake at 350 deg. For 20 minutes. Allow to stand in foil for another 5 minutes.

Serve with rice and Greek salad

Tuna Salad with Curry

1-61/2 0z. Can white tuna
1 tsp. curry pdr.
¼ cup sour cream
¼ cup green onion-chopped
¼ cup raw cauliflower florets- cut into small pieces
Salt/ pepper to taste

Drain and flake tuna with a fork and place in a bowl. Mix curry pdr. With sour cream and add tuna. Fold in the vegetables, gently.
Add salt and pepper to taste,

Serve on a bed of lettuce with tomato wedges and cucumber slices

Serves 2

Baked stuffed Scallops

1 lb. scallops
¼ lb. melted butter
2-½ cups crushed crackers
Salt and pepper
4 strips of bacon-cooked and crumbled

Cut scallops in half (if they are large)
Arrange scallops in casserole dish or pie dish. Mix butter and crackers and spread over scallops. Top off with bacon. Add salt and pepper.
Bake at 350 deg. for about 30 minutes.

Baked Shrimp

¾ lbs shrimp
½ stick margarine- melted
2 tbsp. lemon juice
1 small onion- chopped
Salt/pepper
¼ cup bread crumbs
3 tbsp. crushed almonds

Arrange shrimp in a greased, shallow baking dish. Combine remaining ingredients, except nuts.
Spread mixture over shrimp. Bake At 400 deg. For 20 minutes.
Add almonds during last few minutes of baking.

To crisp off (optional) put under broiler.

(SERVES 3)

Excellent hot or cold!

Shrimp- fresh or thawed shoild be Used the same day--

Fresh shrimp can be frozen up to 3 Months.

Seafood Quiche

2-10 inch pie shells
1-6 oz. pkg. frozen crab meat- thawed and drained
1-½ cups cooked shrimp
8-oz. grated Swiss cheese
½ cup celery-finely chopped
1 cup white wine
½ cup mayonnaise
2 tbsp. flour
4 beaten eggs
1 onion- chopped

In a bowl,
Combine fish, cheese, celery, and onions . In another bowl combine the rest.
Divide mixture between shells. Then pour the liquid over seafood evenly.

Bake time 30-40-minutes at 350 deg.

Tuna Casserole

3-½ cup s casserole macaroni
1-lg. can white tuna
½ cup mayonnaise
1-lg. can cream of mushroom soup
1 cup celery-diced
1 medium onion-chopped
Salt-pepper to taste
1 cup milk (or cream)
1 cup shredded cheddar cheese
1 can mushrooms-- diced and drained

Cook macaroni till tender--drain
Combine macaroni, tuna, mayo, veggies salt and pepper.
In another pot-
Blend soup and milk (or cream) and heat through. Add cheese- stir till
cheese melts. Add   macaroni to mixture. Pour into 1-½ quart casserole dish.
 Bake at 375 for 25 minutes.

*   Noodles can be a substitute for the macaroni

Shrimp Scampi and Spinach fettuccini

1 box spinach pasta
¼ cup -or less- olive oil
1 red pepper-diced
1-½ lbs. frozen shrimp
¼ tsp. minced garlic
Salt/ pepper to taste
¼ cup parsley- chopped
½ stick butter
2. Tbsp. lemon juice

Cook fettuccine as directed. --drain
 Heat oil in lg. skillet on medium heat. Add red pepper and cook until
tender. Add shrimp and cook until pink. Takes only a few minutes. Season
with salt and pepper and remove from heat. Stir in parsley, butter, and lemon
juice. Toss shrimp mixture with drained pasta.
Sprinkle with parmesan cheese

Also great with linguini.

Fish and Veggies cooked in foil

Haddock or scrod- 4 filets
Salt and pepper to taste
1 clove garlic-crushed
2 small zucchini
2 small carrots
2 cups broccoli florets   slice all vegetables
1 lg. onion
1 tomato
2 tbsp. parmesan cheese

Place fish on heavy aluminum foil sprayed with cooking oil.
Salt and pepper to taste. Place veggies on top of fish. Sprinkle with
parmesan cheese. Wrap all together in foil sealing ends tightly.
Bake at 350 deg. For 25-35 minutes. Till veggies are tender and fish is done.

Greek style Fish

All purpose flour
Olive oil
2 lbs. red snapper- cut into quarters
2 lg. white onions
1/2 cup white drinking wine
½ cup water
1 cup tomato sauce
2 tbsp. chopped fresh parsley
2 tbsp. bread crumbs
Salt and pepper to taste
1 garlic clove- finely minced
1 lemon
Sliced tomatoes

Sauté onions and garlic in olive oil until golden brown and tender.
Add wine, water, salt and pepper and tomato sauce.
Simmer on low heat to thicken.   Shut off heat and set aside.
Dredge fish in flour. Fry in olive oil till golden brown on both sides. Put
fish in lightly greased baking dish with slice of tomato on top of each piece.
Squeeze lemon over all.
Add tomato sauce mixture. Sprinkle with bread crumbs and chopped
parsley.
Bake at 350 deg. For 15 minutes. This will thicken the sauce.

Kalamarákia (Greek Squid)

1 lb. Squid- cleaned and boned
Flour-for coating
Salt and pepper
½ cup olive oil
¼ cup white wine
Juice of 1 lemon

Wash Squid thoroughly. Pull out soft back bone and ink sack from head of
each. Remove black membrane from over the entire Squid. Coat them with
flour, salt and pepper.. Fry in olive oil in a heavy skillet until Squid is
golden brown. Pour wine over the Squid. Stir and turn off heat.
Add lemon juice and stir. Allow to stand in sauce for 10 minutes-then drain.
Arrange on a serving platter. Serve with rice and Greek salad.

Simple Fish Batter

1-¼ cups instant Biscuit mix
¾ cup beer
1 egg
¼ tsp. salt

Mix all ingredients together.

Dip fish into batter. Allow to soak for 4-5 minutes. Coat both sides of fish.
Fry fish in oil.
Cook over low heat for 5 minutes on each side till brown

Garides Tourkolimano (Greek Shrimp)

3 lbs. large raw shrimp
½ cup lemon juice
½ butter-whipped
1 garlic clove- minced
1 cup chopped green onions
3 lg. tomatoes-peeled and cut in wedges
1 lb. Feta cheese- crumbled
¾ cup sherry or wine
1 tsp. oregano

Peel and devein shrimp. Add lemon juice. Mix and set aside.
Melt butter in lg. skillet. Sauté garlic, green onions and tomato wedges.
Add shrimp and season with oregano, salt and pepper to taste.
Turn shrimp frequently. Sauté until pink.
Add Feta cheese and wine. Bring to a boil, cook for 3-4 minutes.

Remove shrimp to serving dish . Spoon cheese and wine mixture over
Shrimp.

Shrimp Pilaf

1 clove garlic-minced
1 bunch scallions chopped
¼ cup oil (a little less)
½ lb. shrimp or scallops or clams-cleaned
½ can tomato sauce
1 cup rice
3 cups water
1 tsp. salt
½ tsp. pepper
Parsley-BIG HAND FULL!

In a 4 qt. pot

Sauté garlic and onions in oil till tender.
Mix tomato sauce with 1 cup water and stir. Add remaining water and bring
to a boil. Add rice, salt and pepper--stir once.
Cover and cook on low heat about 30 minutes or until rice is tender.

In skillet

Sauté shrimp in butter till pink//takes only a few minutes.
Add to rice.

Shrimp Jambalaya

1 lb. cooked shrimp
1 cup ham- cubed
1 onion- minced
1 clove garlic-finely chopped
3 tbsp, butter or margarine
3 cups beef broth
1 tbsp. parsley- chopped
Salt and pepper to taste
1 can tomato puree
1 cup rice
1 tsp. Tabasco sauce
¼ tsp. hot red pepper flakes (or more for added heat)

Simmer onion, garlic, salt, pepper and parsley.
Add tomato puree, beef broth and ham. Bring to a boil. Add rice.
Stir occasionally. Cook 25-30 minutes, Add shrimp, Tabasco sauce
And red pepper flakes. Stir and cook for another 10 minutes.
Serve with salad and enjoy..

Fish with a Sweet Touch

Fish sauce

½ cup orange juice
½ cup lemon juice
1 onion finely chopped
½ tsp. lemon zest
1 tsp parsley-chopped

combine ingredients and bring to a boil-simmer for 5 minutes and set aside.

For the fish---

2 lbs. white fish -sliced thin for frying
3 cucumbers-sliced
Margarine
2 kiwi-peeled and sliced

Fry fish in 1 tsp. of oil on med. Heat, covered.

In a separate pan cook cucumber slices in margarine to heat through.
Put cucumbers on a platter, slices of kiwi on top, next the fish and pour
heated sauce over all

.

Fish and Shrimp Bake

2 lbs. frozen Haddock fillets
1 can creamed soup (your choice)
¼ cup butter or margarine
1 small onion-grated
1 tsp. Worcestershire sauce
¼ tsp. garlic pdr.
¼ cup crushed Ritz crackers

Place slightly thawed fish into greased 13x9x2 inch baking dish.
Bake at 375deg. For about 20 minutes. Combine butter, seasonings and
cracker crumbs . Sprinkle over fish. Bake another 10 minutes
  Yummmmm!!

Serves 6

"This is the beginning of a new day. You have been given this day to use as you will. You can waste it or use it for good.

What you do today is important because you are exchanging a day of your life for it. When tomorrow comes, this day will be gone forever, in it's place is something that you have left behind. Let it be something good."

Author unknown

Spices and Herbs Used in Greek Cooking

Bahari --------- Allspice
Glykaniso----- Anise
Roka----------- Arugula
Vasilikos------ Basil
Daphni--------- Bay Leaf
Karthamo---- Cardamom
Garifalo-------- Cloves
Kolianthro--- Coriander
Kymino------ Cumin
Kari----------- Curry
Anithos------- Dill
Maratho------ Fennel Leaves
Piperoriza---- Ginger
Kafteres Piperies- Hot Peppers
Mastiha----- - Mastic
Dyosmos---- Mint
Moustarda Skoni- Mustard Powder
Moschokarido--Nutmeg
Rigani------- Oregano
Maidanos--- Parsley
Piperi------- Pepper
Glistritha--- Purslane
Thentrolivano--Rosemary
Zafora------ Saffron
Faskomilo-- Sage
Estragon---- Tarragon
Selino------ Wild Celery
Vanilia----- Vanila

Sweet Dishes // Desserts

Sweet Dishes And Desserts

Sandwich Nut Bread
Chocolate Chip Cookies
Date Nut Bread
Nutty S'mores---(every kids favorite)
Mom's Homemade Fudge
Tiganides-----Greek Medallion Pancakes or Fritters
Banana Nut Muffins
Koulourakia----Greek Cookie Twists
Indian Pudding
Cheese Puffs
Spinach Puffs
Zucchini Bread
Fruity Cream Puffs
Lemony Bars
Gooey Butter Cakes
Karidopita-----Greek Walnut Cake
Tyropita---Feta Cheese Filled Pastry
Fudge Squares
Dreamy Date Bars
Rizogalo----Rice Pudding
Strawberry Raspberry Mold
Baklava-------Flaky, Nutty, Sweet Honey Pastry
Stuffed -Butter Baked Apples
Candied Dried Fruit
Bourekakia----Honey Nut Rolls
Halva------Sweet Pastry
Pound Cake Delight with Fruit
Frosted Walnuts
Fudgie Bars
Fruity Yogurt Milkshake
Spanakopeta------Spinach Pie
Pineapple Zucchini Bread
Tyropita------Cheese Pie (Favorite Snack in Greece)
Galatoboureko------Greek Custard-Baked in Filo
Brandy Ice Cream
Speedy Spinach Pie

Sweet Dishes And Desserts

Melomakarona-----Greek- Honey Dipped Spice Cookie
               (A Christmas Tradition)
Chocolaty Brownies
Paximadia-------Greek Toast Cookies
Apple Raisin Crisp
Kourambiedes----Greek Christmas Cookie
Peanut Butter and Chocolate Dream Pie
Banana Bread Pudding
Nutty Loaf
Chewy Chocolate Macaroons
Fresh Carrot Cake---(Lenten)
Chocolate Nut Cake (Lenten)
Diples-------Deep Fried Greek Honey Rolls
Coffee Cake Muffins
Loukoumades------Greek Donuts
Kolliva----(Sitare)   Wheat For Memorial Services
Lemon Cake Supreme
Lemon Cheese Cake
Blueberry Cheese Cake
Carrot Cake
Bread Pudding
Strawberry Afternoon Delight
Deep -Dark Chocolate Cookies
Paximadia----Greek Walnut Cookie Slices
Banana Split Cake
Apple Coffee Cake
Squash Pie
Mom's Early American Pear Pie
Strawberry Jello Cheese Cake
Pear or Apple Crumble

Sandwich Nut Bread

3 cups flour-sifted
3 tsp. baking powder
1 tsp. salt
¾ cup sugar
1 cup nuts- chopped
2 eggs - well beaten
1-¼ cup milk
4 tbsp. butter - melted

Sift flour once, add baking powder, salt and sugar and sift again.
Add nuts and mix well.
Combine eggs and milk, add to dry ingredients and blend.
Add melted butter and stir.

Bake in greased loaf pan 8x4x3 inches @ 350 deg. oven for about 1 hour and 15 minutes or until done.

** Store bread for several hours (over night is best) before slicing.

Chocolate Chip Cookies

2-¼ cups flour
½ tsp. baking soda ---   Mix together

1 egg
1 cup margarine or butter
1 cup sugar
12 oz. pkg. chocolate chips
½ cup walnuts- chopped
1-½ tsp. vanilla

Cream together the sugar and butter.
Add egg and vanilla. Gradually add the flour and baking soda. Mix until completely incorporated. Add walnuts and chocolate chips. Mix well.

Drop teaspoonful (heaping) onto cookie sheet. (don't crowd them)
Bake @ 350 deg. For 10-15 minutes until golden brown.

Date Nut Bread

1 egg
1-½ cups flour
1 cup sugar
1 pkg. dates-chopped
1 cup walnuts-chopped
1 tsp. vanilla
1 tbsp. butter
1 tsp. baking soda

Put baking soda over dates- add 1 cup boiling water and let stand until cooled.
Cream sugar, butter, egg , walnuts and vanilla.
Add date mixture and flour and mix well.

Bake 45-50 minutes @325 to 350 deg.

** makes 1 loaf

Nutty S'mores --- (every kids favorite)

Graham crackers
Chocolate bars
Marshmallows
½ cup walnuts-finely chopped

Place the marshmallows on a pan lined with foil. Broil until nicely hot and brown. Then assemble the crackers, chocolate, nuts and marshmallows. The marshmallows will melt the chocolate and become a gooey , finger licking Delight.

***FYI--loved by grown ups too!!

Mom's   Homemade Fudge

2 tbsp. butter
2 squares chocolate---or 8 tbsp. cocoa
2 cups sugar (or less)
¾ cup milk
½ tsp. vanilla
¼ cup walnuts-chopped

Combine all ingredients in a saucepan except the vanilla.
Boil till thick, stirring almost constantly. At that point, try dropping a tiny
amount from a spoon, into cold water and if it forms a soft ball, It's done. If
not, continue to boil and try again until it does.

 Then add vanilla and walnuts and stir. Pour into pan and spread it out
evenly.

Allow to cool and cut into small squares.

Tiganides---Greek Medallion Pancakes or Fritters

3 eggs	1-½ tsp. salt
1-½ cup warm water	8-10 cups flour--unsifted
1 cup warm milk	2 tbsp. sugar (or less if desired)
½ cup melted butter	
½ cup oil	
1 pkgs. Dry yeast	

Dissolve yeast in ½ cup water and 1 tsp. sugar and mix well.--set aside--

In lg. bowl, combine eggs, warm water, milk, butter, oil, salt and yeast.
Mix until well blended.

Add flour (as much as needed to make a dough)
Mix with hand and knead until smooth as silk. Cover dough with dry cloth
and allow to rise until it's doubled in size. (several hours)

Cut dough in small pieces and roll like small logs. Let them rise again until
doubled in size.

Put 2 inches of oil in lg. frying pan. Fry dough in hot oil till golden brown .
On both sides.

Drain on paper towels   Makes about 3 dozen

**Serve with feta cheese   Fantastic any time----

Banana Nut Muffins

1 egg
2 cups Bisquick baking mix
1 cup mashed ,ripe bananas
¼ cup sugar
2 tbsp. milk
2 tbsp. vegetable oil
1 cup walnuts--finely chopped---optional

Pre-heat oven @ 400 deg.

Grease bottom of 12 medium muffin cups or line with baking cups.

Beat egg slightly. Stir in remaining ingredients until well incorporated. Pour equal amount of batter into each cup.
 Bake until golden brown.--15-17 minutes

Makes 12 muffins

Koulourákia ----Greek Cookie Twists

1 lb. butter	4 lbs. flour----approximately
½ cup Crisco	2-½ cups sugar
12 eggs	3 tbsp. vanilla
7 tsp. baking powder	

Beat butter and Crisco for 15 minutes. Add sugar and beat another 5 minutes.
Add eggs, one at a time beating thoroughly. Add vanilla.

Stir flour and baking powder and add to mixture one cup at a time.

** dough must be soft--not stiff.

Add 3 tbsp. whiskey (optional) and knead the dough well.
Roll into braided cookies---shapes are optional
Brush tops of cookies with beaten egg whites.

Bake @ 350 deg. In pre-heated oven until lightly brown

*** you can also form cookies into donut shapes

This is an Easter specialty!

Indian Pudding

4 cups milk
½ cup yellow corn meal
2 tbsp. margarine--melted
½ cup molasses
1 tsp. salt
1 tsp. cinnamon
¼ tsp. ginger
2 eggs
hard sauce

To make hard sauce-----

1/3 cup margarine
1 cup confectioner's sugar
1 tsp. vanilla

Cream the margarine. Add confectioner's sugar (make fluffy) Add vanilla and mix.

To make pudding----

Scald milk and pour slowly over corn meal. Stir constantly.. Cook over hot water for about 20 minutes.
Combine margarine, molasses, salt, cinnamon, and ginger. Beat eggs well and add, with molasses mixture ,to the corn meal.

Pour into greased baking dish. Place in pan with hot water. Bake @ 300 deg. For 1 hour.

** Serve hot with hard sauce or whipped cream and ice cream

Cheese Puffs

½ lb. grated feta cheese
1-3 oz. pkg. cream cheese
2 eggs- beaten
½ pint ricotta cheese
dash of nutmeg
8 filo sheets
2 sticks butter

Beat eggs and cheese in a bowl till creamy. Add nutmeg and mix.
Cut filo sheets in 4x8 pieces. Brush with butter . Place ½ tsp. cheese and
roll up. Bake @ 350 deg. Till golden brown.

Spinach Puffs

1 pkg. frozen, chopped spinach-drained
3 tbsp. olive oil
1 onion- finely chopped
¼ lb. feta cheese
4 oz. cottage cheese
1 egg

Sauté onion in olive oil until soft. Remove from heat and add spinach.
Mix cheeses and beaten egg. Blend together well. Cut filo in 4s buttering
the pieces.
 Add the filling and roll up. (don't over fill the pieces)

Bake @ 375 deg. Till golden brown.

Zucchini Bread

4 eggs
1-¼ cups Crisco (No other will do)
3 cups sugar
2 tsp. vanilla
4 cups zucchini- grated
4 cups flour
1 cup cocoanut- shredded
¾ cup walnuts-chopped
½ cup raisins
2 tsp. baking powder
2 t sp. Baking soda
2 tsp. cinnamon

Beat eggs . Add oil , sugar and vanilla. Mix well. Add zucchini.
Combine dry ingredients and add to egg mixture.

Pour into 2 greased, floured loaf pans.
Bake @ 360 deg. For 1 hour to 1 hour and 10 minutes.

** makes 2 big loaves

Fruity Cream Puffs

1pkg. Stella Doro puffs- or similar
1 8 oz. pkg. cream cheese
1- 20 oz. can crushed pineapples-drained
1-8 oz. container cool whip

Whip the cream cheese, cool whip and crushed pineapples
Cool in fridge. Fill cream puffs.

Place in refrigerator for a few hours before serving.

** cut puffs with sharp knife--not serated

Lemony Bars

¾ cup butter
1-½ cups- plus 3 tbsp. flour (separate amounts)
½ cup confectioner's sugar
½ cup sugar
3 eggs- slightly beaten
Juice from 1 lemon

Mix butter, 1-½ cups flour and confectioner's sugar.
Spread into a 9x 13 inch pan.
Bake @ 350 deg. For 20 minutes

In a bowl- add sugar, 3 tbsp. flour and lemon juice to eggs and mix well.
Pour over hot crust and bake 20 minutes longer.
Sprinkle with powdered sugar while hot.

Allow to cool before cutting into bars.

** Serve with fruit or ice cream or just plain is great!

Gooey Butter Cakes

1 yellow cake mix
2 eggs
1 stick butter-melted
1-8oz. pkg. cream cheese-softened
½ cup plain peanut butter
1 box powdered sugar
1 banana- smashed
½ tsp. vanilla

Mix together--

1 box yellow cake mix
1 egg
1 stick butter-melted

Batter will be thick.
Put in baking pan.

Blend--

1-8oz. pkg. softened cream cheese with ½ cup plain peanut butter
Add1 box powdered sugar, 1 egg, 1 smashed banana, and ½ tsp. vanilla
Pour over dough.

Bake @350 deg. For 45-50 minutes.

** They will be gooey and delish!

Karidopita-------Greek Walnut Cake

1 cup butter
1-½ cups sugar
2-½ cups flour
1 cup walnuts-finely chopped
5 eggs
1 tsp. cinnamon
2 tsp. baking powder

   For the syrup----
Boil 2-¾ cups water, and 1-¾ cups sugar for 10 minutes and cool.--set aside.

Cream butter with sugar until well blended. Add eggs, one at a time , beating well after each addition.

Combine dry ingredients slowly and stir in walnuts.

Grease 10x 14 pan. Pour in mixture and bake @425 deg. For 30 minutes or until cake springs back at touch of finger.

Pour cooled syrup over hot cake. When cooled, cut into diamond or square shapes.

** This is a decadent dessert!

Tyrópita------Feta Cheese Filled Pastry

1 lb. Feta cheese-crumbled
2 egg yolks
2 eggs
4 tbsp. parsley- chopped
Pepper
¾ lb. butter--melted and kept warm
1 lb. filo dough- (keep covered with damp cloth, not to dry out)

In a bowl--
Mash feta cheese with a fork. Add egg yolks, whole eggs, parsley and
pepper. Mix till well incorporated.
Melt butter in saucepan. Keep on stove on very low heat.

Lay out a sheet of filo dough. Brush well with butter. Cut in 2 inch wide
strips.
Put a heaping teaspoonful of mixture on each strip. Fold into a triangle.
Continue until all the triangles are made.

Place all pieces on a sprayed baking sheet. Bake @ 350 deg. For 20
minutes. till golden brown.

** makes 8-10 pieces

Fudge Squares

2 squares unsweetened chocolate (2 oz.)
¼ cup margarine
1 cup sugar
1-1/4 cups bisquick mix
2 eggs
½ cups walnuts--chopped

Pre-heat oven to 350 deg.

Melt chocolate and butter together. Mix in sugar, eggs ,bisquick mix and
Nuts. Spread in greased 8x8 x2 or 9x9 x2 pan.

Bake for 30-35 minutes. Do not over bake. Cool and cover with topping.

Topping------

¼ cup margarine
1 tbsp. milk
2 cups sifted confectioner's sugar
1 tsp. vanilla
1-½ squares semi-sweet chocolate

Cream together ¼ cup margarine, 1 tbsp. milk, 2 cups sifted confectioner's
sugar, and 1 tsp. vanilla. Spread over cooled squares. Melt 1-½ squares of
semi-sweet chocolate. Spread evenly over top. After chocolate hardens, cut
into squares.

Dreamy Date Bars

2 eggs
1 tbsp. butter-melted
¼ tsp. salt
1 cups dates--chopped
1 tsp. vanilla
1 cup confectioner's sugar
¼ cup sifted cake flour
¾ cup walnuts--chopped
¼ tsp. baking powder

Beat eggs until light . Add sugar and butter. Blend well.
Sift dry ingredients together and add dates, nuts and vanilla. Blend well and
pour into greased, shallow cake pan. Bake @ 325 deg. About 25-30
minutes. Cool.-- Cut bars and roll in confectioner's sugar.

Rizógalo   -----Rice Pudding

8 cups milk
1 cup rice
1-½ cups sugar
1 tsp. corn starch
1 lemon rind
1 tbsp. cinnamon
2 egg yolks

In a sauce pan -bring milk to a boil. Add rice to the milk. At the boiling point again, lower heat and simmer for about 30 minutes or until cooked. Stir occasionally. Add sugar, lemon rind, 2 egg yolks (mixed with a little cold milk) and corn starch. Simmer for a few minutes longer.

Remove lemon rind before serving. Serve in separate dessert cups.

When cooled, sprinkle cinnamon on top-----and enjoy!!

Strawberry Raspberry Mold

3 pkgs. Raspberry Jell-O
1 pkg. frozen strawberries
1 can crushed pineapples- drained
2 bananas- sliced
½ pint sour cream

Dissolve Jell-O in 2-½ cups boiling water.
Add 2 cups room temperature water. Let set in freezer for ¾ of an hour.
Whip in strawberries, pineapples (no liquid) and bananas.
Pour half of the mixture in a mold and layer with sour cream and remaining
jell-o mixture on top.

Set in refrigerator over night.

Baklavá-----Flaky, Nutty, Sweet Honey Pastry

¾ cup finely chopped walnut	1 tsp. cinnamon
¾ cup finely chopped pistachios	1 tsp. nutmeg
½ cup chopped, blanched almonds	5 whole cloves
2-½ cups sugar	1 cinnamon stick
1-¾ cups water	1 cup honey
1 orange rind- finely grated	½ cup super fine sugar
1 lemon rind-finely grated	1-¼ lb. sweet butter
1 pkg. commercial Filo sheets	(melted)

** almonds should be lightly toasted---

Combine nuts, sugar, cinnamon and nutmeg. Brush a 13 x 9 x 2 inch baking pan well with butter.
Place 1 filo sheet in pan and trim to fit. Brush generously with melted butter.
Repeat procedure until there are 5 layers of buttered filo in the pan.

Sprinkle with ¼ of the nut mixture. Repeat this procedure 2 more times, ending with filo.
Drizzle any remaining butter over top.

Bake in 350 deg. Oven for 1-½ hours or until golden brown.

Remove from oven . Using a sharp knife , immediately cut long ,diagonal lines from corner to corner, forming an X. Follow these guidelines to cut the pastry into serving sized diamonds . While still hot pour cooled syrup over Baklava.

   To Make Syrup-------

Combine sugars ,water, orange and lemon rinds, cloves and cinnamon stick in saucepan. Bring to a boil and simmer, uncovered for about 5 minutes to thicken slightly . Remove from heat, remove spices and stir in honey.
 Cool to room temp. and pour over hot pastry.

** Allow to stand over night before serving.

Stuffed-Butter Baked Apples

4 apples---Grannie smith or McIntosh
Cinnamon
½ cup raisins
½ cup honey
½ cup almonds---or walnuts-chopped
4-½ tsp. butter

Put the nuts, raisins and honey in bowl and mix well.
Core the apples and place them close together in a well buttered bake pan .

Fill apples with stuffing. Drizzle honey to top off.
Sprinkle top of apples with sugar and cinnamon. Add 4 tbsp. water to
the pan and bake at 350 deg. until apples are soft and bubbly. (not falling
apart)

Allow to stand for 5 minutes, and serve with vanilla ice cream

**   Any liquid remaining in the bottom of the pan can be used as a sauce to
pour over all.

Candied Dried Fruit

1 lg. bag mixed dried fruit
orange juice
1 strip lemon peel

In a sauce pan, cover the fruit with orange juice. Add the lemon peel. Cover and simmer on low heat for about 30 minutes until the juice is absorbed and the fruit plumps up.
Remove lemon peel.

Serve warm or cold

Bourekákia----Honey Nut Rolls

Filling---

2 cups-or more- chopped nut
(almonds, pecans, walnuts, pistachio, or any combination)
¼ cup sugar
½ tsp. cinnamon
1 orange (rind only) -grated   Syrup----
½ lb. commercial filo sheets
½ lb. sweet butter   2 cups honey
                                      1 cup water
                                      1 tbsp. lemon juice
                                      2 cups sugar

Filo sheets should defrost for at least 2 hours before using.
Mix filling in a bowl and set aside. Melt butter in a separate pan.

**If necessary-reheat butter to keep it a bit warm and easier to work with.

Layer 3 filo sheets on a flat surface - brushing warm butter between each
sheet. Cover completely. Sprinkle 2/3 cup on nut filling over top and
corners. Layer another 3 sheets of filo over the filling , buttering between
each sheet. Continue process until all the filling is used up . Fold edges
over to keep nut filling from falling out.

Start rolling up from the end nearest you and continue rolling as tightly as
you can. Cut into one inch pieces and place them on an oiled cooking pan,
nut side up.
Drizzle a little warm butter over each one.

Bake @ 350 deg. For 45 minutes.

Make syrup about 15 minutes before pastry is finished cooking.
Pour hot syrup, immediately over all the pieces.

Allow to rest in the syrup for 4 hours.
    ** Do not refrigerate

Halva----Sweet Pastry

2 cups farina
¾ cups butter--at room temperature
1 cup sugar
1 cup walnuts- chopped
4 eggs
1 tsp. cinnamon

Syrup

2 cups sugar   ----   Boil sugar and water until sugar is
4 cups water   completely dissolved. Pour on top
                              of pastry immediately after baking

Cream butter, add sugar and blend well. Add eggs, one at a time, incorporate well. Add farina, walnuts and cinnamon.

Use a 3 inch deep , greased baking dish.
Bake @ 35 deg. For 35-40 minutes
 Pour syrup over top.

Allow to cool before cutting into squares.

   ** Serve with tea or coffee

Pound Cake Delight with Fruit

2 cups flour
1 stick margarine
3 eggs
2 tbsp. baking pdr.
1 cup sugar
½ tsp. salt
1 cup milk
1-½ tsp. vanilla
1 pkg. assorted frozen fruit--thawed
Whipped cream

Mix all dry ingredients together. Melt margarine.
Beat eggs slightly. Add melted margarine and eggs to dry ingredients .
Then add milk and mix together. Add vanilla.

Bake @350 deg. For 45-50 minutes .

Allow to cool completely before slicing. Top off each slice with fruit and whipped cream.

Frosted Walnuts

½ cup sour cream
1-½ cups sugar
1-½ tsp. vanilla
4 cups walnuts

Boil sour cream, sugar and vanilla to soft ball stage. Pour over nuts and mix.
Spread out on a greased cookie sheet and allow to set .
Break into pieces.

** Great treat !!

Fudgie Bars

2-½ cups flour
2 cups sugar
¾ cups cocoa
½ tsp. salt
1 tsp. baking soda
2 eggs--unbeaten
2/3 cup + ¼ cup oil
1-½ tsp. vanilla
1-½ cup cold water
1 cup--or more- chopped nuts-chopped
1 pkg. chocolate chips

Stir all dry ingredients together. Add oil, eggs, water, and vanilla.
Beat thoroughly for a thin batter.

Use an 11x17 inch ungreased pan. Sprinkle chopped nuts and chocolate
chips on top.

Bake @ 350 deg. for 30 minutes. Allow to cool and cut into bars.

Fruity Yogurt Milkshake

1 cup plain yogurt
1 cup sliced strawberries
1 cup milk
1 lg. banana-ripened
2 tbsp. sugar
pinch of cinnamon
2 tbsp. strawberry ice cream--optional

Put all ingredients in blender--till frothy

** refreshing to say the least!!

Spanakópeta----Spinach Pie

2 lbs. filo sheets--- allow to defrost at least 4 hours before using
1 lb. butter---melted and warm
2 pkgs. fresh spinach---wash, remove stems and chop into small pieces
1-½ lbs. Feta cheese --crumbled
12 eggs--slightly beaten
1-2 bunches scallions--finely chopped

** Requires 15inch to 17 inch round pan

Filling--
In a lg. bowl add beaten eggs, spinach, scallions, crumbled Feta cheese and
¼ of the melted butter.
Mix until all ingredients are well incorporated. (hands are your best tools)

Wipe peta pan generously with oil. Start with 4 filo sheets on bottom of pan.
Layer them in a circular design, Covering entire bottom.
Brush entire filo with melted butter. Repeat with 2 more filo sheets.

Add a little spinach mixture evenly to cover bottom of pan.
Repeat with 2 more filo sheets. Brush with warm butter.
Repeat with 2 more filo and add spinach mixture.

Continue this process until all the mixture is gone ending with
6 filo sheets on top and brushed with butter.
Roll and fold the edges of dough around the pan.

Bake @ 350 deg. For about 50-60 minutes or until golden brown.
Allow to cool thoroughly.
Cut into diamond or square shapes.

**can be refrigerated

Pineapple Zucchini Bread

1 cup raisins	¾ tsp. nutmeg
3 eggs- beaten	3 cups flour
1 cup oil	2 tsp. baking soda
2 cups sugar	1 tsp. salt
2 tsp. vanilla	½ tsp. baking pdr.

2 cups zucchini- coarsely shredded
1-8oz. can crushed pineapple-drained
1-½ tsp. cinnamon
1 cup walnuts-chopped

Combine eggs, oil, sugar, and vanilla in a bowl and beat until thick.
Add zucchini and pineapple and mix well.

Combine flour, baking soda, salt, baking powder and spices and add to
zucchini mixture, stirring until moistened.
Pour into two greased, floured loaf pans.
Bake @ 350 deg. for 1 hour and cool before slicing.

Tyrópita---Cheese Pie (Favorite Snack in Greece)

1 lb. Feta cheese
4 tbsp. butter
6 eggs
½ cup parsley-chopped
15 sheets filo dough
3 cups white Béchamel sauce
Salt, pepper, grated nutmeg

Place cheese in a bowl and crush into a paste. Add white sauce and blend.
Add eggs, one at a time, stirring well. Add salt, pepper, nutmeg and parsley.
  Mix thoroughly.
Line buttered baking pan with 5-6 sheets of filo. Sprinkle melted butter on
each sheet.
Pour cheese batter and spread evenly with a spatula.

Cover with the rest of the filo sheets, sprinkling with melted butter in
between each sheet.

Trim pastry around the pan before adding the last filo sheet. Fold over the
edges . Brush surface with melted butter, and with a sharp knife trace the top
sheet into square pieces about 3 inches wide from the end of the pan to the
other, and then cross wise.

Bake @ 350 deg. For 45 minutes or till golden brown.

  Cool, cut and serve.

Galatoboúreko   ---Greek Custard- Baked in Filo

10-15 sheets filo dough

Filling---

8 cups milk	7 eggs
2 cups sugar	1 cup butter
1-½ cups farina	2 tbsp. vanilla
Grated rind of 1 orange	

Syrup---

1-½ lbs. sugar
3 cups water ---------- Bring to a boil and set aside

Heat milk in a lg. saucepan, add sugar, orange rind and vanilla. When near boiling, slowly add farina ,stirring constantly, till smooth.

Remove from heat , stir occasionally to allow cooling and prevent forming a crust.
When just lukewarm, add eggs, one at a time, mixing constantly.
Line the bottom of a greased baking pan with a sheet of filo, bringing it over the edges of the pan. Brush with melted butter.

Continue same process, basting each sheet until you've used half of them.
Add cream filling -spread evenly. Cover entire surface with remaining sheets basting each one with melted butter.
Trim the edges- Score the top of the sheet with a knife in diamond or square shapes.
Bake @ 350 deg. For about 40-45 minutes till golden brown.

So Delicious!!

Brandy Ice Cream

1 qt. good quality vanilla ice cream --softened
3 oz. brandy
½ cup walnuts --chopped
1 banana--small pieces
½ cup cherries chopped

Mix altogether, refreeze and serve

Speedy Spinach Pie

3 eggs
2 cups milk
½ lb. feta cheese
2 cups Bisquick mix
1 stick butter-melted
1-10 oz. pkg. frozen spinach-defrosted
Few scallions-chopped

Pre-heat oven---@350 deg.

Beat eggs, add milk, Bisquick mix and spinach. Mix together well.
Add feta cheese and scallions.

Pour into a 9x13 pan and pour melted butter on top.
Bake @ 350 deg. For 40-45 minutes .

Melomakárona-----Greek- Honey Dipped Spice Cookie
(A Christmas Tradition)

12 cups flour -sifted

3 cups olive oil

2 cups sugar

1 cup water--room temp

1 cup walnuts- finely chopped

5 tbsp. vanilla

juice and grated peel of 1 orange

2 heaping tsp. baking powder

1 tsp. baking soda

½ tbsp. cinnamon

Syrup---

2 cups water   1 cup honey   --------- Bring to a boil and

4 cups sugar   ½ tbsp. cinnamon   simmer a few minutes
                                                 Set aside.

Beat oil , sugar, orange juice, grated peel and water until completely blended. Add vanilla and mix well.

Add1 cup flour with baking powder , baking soda and chopped walnuts. Mix well.
Continue to add flour, one cup at a time, till all combined and making a soft dough. Knead by hand for about 5 minutes.
Allow dough to sit for 30 minutes.

Make cookies in the shape of eggs.
Bake @ 350 deg. For about 30 minute--allow to cool completely.
Dip in hot syrup soaking them well. Sprinkle with walnuts on top.

Chocolaty Brownies

1 cup sugar
½ cup shortening
2 eggs
1-½ squares unsweetened chocolate -melted
1/3 tsp. salt
½ cup flour
1 cup walnuts-chopped
3 tbsp. boiling water
1 tsp. vanilla

Cream sugar and shortening . Add eggs and beat well until blended and light in color. Add melted chocolate, salt and vanilla and stir till thoroughly blended.
Add boiling water and stir. Add flour and blend. (don't over mix) Pour into 8 inch square, greased pan and sprinkle with confectioner's sugar.
Bake @ 325 deg. For 35 minutes or till just a slight imprint remains with a finger touch.

Paximadia---Greek Toast Cookies

1 cup butter
1 cup sugar
1 tbsp. almonds-grated or finely chopped
3 lg. eggs-beaten
3 tsp. baking powder
51/2 cups flour
½ cup walnuts-chopped
¼ cup milk
1 tbsp. vanilla
½ tsp. baking soda

Use an electric mixer---

Cream butter and sugar. Stir in nuts. Add eggs and mix well.
Add remaining ingredients and blend thoroughly.
Pour into greased 13-½ x 9 inch pan. Bake in pre-heated oven@ 350 deg.
For about 25 minutes or until toothpick inserted comes out clean.

Turn over onto cutting board and slice lengthwise in 3 strips. Then slice in
¾ inch pieces.

** Great for dunking in coffee or tea.

Apple Raisin Crisp

4 cups peeled, sliced apples
¾ cup packed brown sugar
½ cup flour
½ cup oats
¾ tsp. cinnamon
¾ tsp. nutmeg
1/3 cup margarine
1 cup raisins

Pre-heat oven @ 375 deg.

Use an 8x8x2 inch oven pan
Arrange apples in greased pan. Sprinkle raisins on top.
Mix ingredients and spread over apples.
Bake until apples are fork tender and topping is golden brown--about 30
minutes.

** Serve warm with ice cream---   A dream dessert!!

Kourambiedes----Greek Christmas Cookies

1 cup sweet butter
½ cup powdered Sugar
1 egg yolk
2 tbsp. brandy (optional)
1 tsp. almond extract
2-¼ cups cake flour-sifted
1 tsp. baking powder
1 cup almonds-crushed
1 lb. powdered sugar-sifted
1 tsp. vanilla

With electric mixer beat sweet butter until smooth. Reduce speed and slowly add powdered sugar, egg yolk, brandy, almond extract and vanilla.

Sift the baking powder with the flour and slowly add to the batter, a little at a time, till completely incorporated.
Add and mix in the almonds.

Knead the dough until it stays together. Roll pieces of dough into balls the size of golf balls or little foot ball shapes.

Place on cookie sheet with enough space between them. (not crowded)

Bake @ 350 deg. For about 12 minutes or until lightly golden brown.

Place cookies on a sheet of powdered sugar and immediately sift powdered sugar all over top.

Cool completely before plating.

Peanut Butter and Chocolate Dream Pie

1-9 inch chocolate cookie crust
1-8 oz. pkg. cream cheese- softened
¼ cup milk
¾ cup plain peanut butter
1 cup powdered sugar
1- 9 oz. container whipped cream
1/2 cup chocolate-shaved

Combine sugar and softened cream cheese. Add peanut butter and
Milk. Mix well.
Fold in whipped cream and sprinkle chocolate shavings generously all over
top.

Chill for at least 3 hours before cutting.

Banana Bread Pudding

2-½ cups whole milk
2 eggs-slightly beaten
2 bananas- sliced
2-½ cups day old crusty bread-cut in 1 inch cubes
½ cup brown sugar
½ tsp. cinnamon
1 tsp. vanilla
¼ tsp. salt
½ cup seedless raisins

Combine eggs and milk- Pour over bread. Allow to soak for about 1 hour. Mix in remaining ingredients. Pour mixture into a baking dish. Place dish in a shallow pan and pour hot water around it about 1 inch deep.

Bake @ 350 deg. For about 45 minutes or until knife inserted in center comes out clean.

Drizzle hot maple syrup on top of each piece.

Great hot or cold!!

Another topping option:---

Cut strawberries in half and marinate in maple syrup in fridge overnight. Then heat and serve on top of bread pudding.

Nutty Loaf

3 cups flour-sifted
¾ cups sugar
3-½ tsp. baking powder
1 tsp. salt
1 egg-beaten
1-½ cup milk
2 tbsp. oil
¾ cups nuts-chopped

Stir together all dry ingredients. Combine eggs, milk and oil.
Add to dry ingredients. Mix well.

Stir in nuts and pour into greased 9-1/2x5x3 inch loaf pan.
Bake @ 350 deg. for about 1 hour.

Chewy Chocolate Macaroons

1 pkg. - 14 0z. cocoanut
1 can - 14 oz. sweetened condensed milk
2 tsp. vanilla
4 squares unsweetened chocolate- melted

Combine all ingredients in a bowl. Drop from teaspoon, one inch apart on well greased baking sheets. Bake @ 350 deg. For 10-12 minutes

Remove from baking sheets immediately.

** Makes about 8 dozen--
Recipe can be cut in half.

Fresh Carrot Cake---(Lenten)

9x12 greased pan-- lined with wax paper.
3 cups flour
2 cups sugar   1-½ cups water
1 tsp. baking soda.   2/3 cup vegetable oil
2 tsp. cinnamon   2 tsp. vanilla
½ tsp salt   1 cup nuts-chopped
2 cups shredded carrots
3 tbsp. lemon juice

In a lg. mixing bowl combine the flour, sugar, baking soda, cinnamon and salt. Add carrots and mix well.

In another mixing bowl combine lemon juice, water, oil and vanilla.

Add liquid ingredients to dry ingredients mixing well. Stir in nuts.

Pour batter into prepared pan and bake @ 350 deg. For 50-60- minutes or till done.
Cool 10 minutes and remove from pan. Cool right side up and frost.

    Frosting----

Mix 2 cup confectioner's sugar with 4 tbsp. water and ¼ tsp. vanilla.
Drizzle over cooled cake and cut into squares or bars and serve.

        ****Lent lasts from Ash Wednesday to Vespers.
           There are traditionally 40 days in lent which are
          marked by fasting both from foods and festivities.
             Greek Easter must fall after Passover. ****

Chocolate Nut Cake---(Lenten)

9x12 inch pan--greased and lined with wax paper

3 cups flour
2 cups sugar   2 cups water
4 tbsp. cocoa   2 tbsp. cider vinegar
2 tsp. baking soda   1 tsp. vanilla
1 cup vegetable oil   ½ tsp. salt
powdered sugar

Pre-heat oven @ 350 deg.

In a lg. bowl combine all ingredients till well blended. Pour into baking pan. Bake for 45 minutes. Remove from oven to a rack and let stand for 10 minutes. Remove from pan and cool right side up until cold.

Remove wax paper. Sprinkle with powdered sugar. Cut into squares or bars.

*** Frosting option---

Combine 2 cups confectioner's sugar
 3 tbsp. cocoa,
 4 tbsp. water
 ¼ tsp. vanilla

Spread over top
 Sprinkle chopped nuts on top.

Diples----Deep Fried Greek Honey Rolls

To make syrup---

2 cups honey
1 cup water
2 tbsp. sugar

Boil all ingredients for about 15 minutes. Set aside and keep warm.--

-To make pastry---

12 eggs
1 tsp. vanilla
 flour
Cinnamon
¾ cup almonds-crushed
juice of small orange

Beat eggs for about 15 minutes. Add orange juice and then
 add flour, a little at a time, as much as it takes, until it forms a soft dough.--
(Do not make dough stiff.) - Cut dough into sections. Roll out each piece
of dough till thin and cut into squares.

Roll each piece in the shape of a log-or donut (optional)
And fry in hot, deep oil.
Remove when dough is light brown and puffy.

Drain on paper towels. When completely cooled dip each one in prepared
honey syrup and add cinnamon, sugar and crushed nuts on top.

***Can also be fried in square shapes--

Coffee Cake Muffins

1-½ cup flour-sifted
½ cup sugar
2 tsp. baking powder
½ tsp. salt
¼ cup shortening
1 egg- beaten
½ cup milk

Sift dry ingredients in a bowl. Cut in shortening - till mixture is crumbly.
Blend in the egg and milk.
Add all at once to flour mixture. Stir till moist.

Alternate layers of batter and spicy nuts in greased muffin pan. Fill 2/3 full.

To make spicy nuts--

Combine ---½ cup brown sugar
           ½ cup chopped walnuts
           2 tbsp. flour
           2 tsp. cinnamon
           2 tbsp. melted butter

Bake @375 deg. About 20 minutes-

                              Makes 12 muffins

Loukoumádes------Greek Donuts

3 cups water-warm
4 cups flour
1 cup milk
1 pkg. dry yeast
2 eggs-beaten
1 tsp. vanilla
Vegetable oil

To make syrup--

1 cup water
2 cups honey
1 cup sugar
cinnamon

Dissolve yeast in lg. bowl in 2 cups warm water. Let stand for 5 minute.
Add 2 cups flour to yeast and whisk well .
Add eggs and milk till well blended. Add remaining flour and vanilla.

Batter will be a thick consistency.
Cover bowl--allow to rise for 2 hours.

Syrup--
In a small pan mix sugar , honey and water. Bring to a boil then simmer to dissolve the sugar.

Heat oil to about 350 deg. Drop in batter with a spoon. Dough will rise to the surface.
Cook till golden brown, remove and drain on paper towels.

Dip them, one by one, in the syrup and sprinkle with cinnamon.

** Delicious-- served hot!

Kóllyva ----(Sitare)   Wheat For Memorial Services

**Cook 2 days before using--and assemble the day of the service.

1 cup shelled wheat   1 tsp. cinnamon
1/8 cup granulated sugar   ½ cup powered sugar
¼ cup slivered almonds   ½ cup finely ground zwieback
¼ cup walnuts-finely chopped   toast
½ cup raisins-white
¼ lb. colored almonds (koufeta)

Clean and wash wheat thoroughly. Soak for 4-5 hours. Drain and rinse. Put
in boiling water and cook for at least 3-4 hours- till wheat becomes puffy.

Drain and rinse in cold water a few times.
Spread the wheat onto a sheet and dry over night.

In a bowl combine all ingredients except the powdered sugar , Zwieback
crumbs, slivered nuts and decorations.
Cover tray with wax paper. Put mixture on serving tray molding it into a
mound, higher in the center- pressing it until smooth.

Spread crumbs all over top covering the wheat thoroughly and press firmly.
Cover mound with sifted powderd sugar . (use a sifter)
 Press firmly using wax paper.

Make the sign of the cross in center of mound with candy colored
Almonds. (koufeta)--

Use the slivered almonds to make the initial of the first name of the
deceased on the left of the cross, and the initial of the last name on the
right.

Lemon Cake Supreme

1 pkg. lemon jello -small   Filling mixture
¾ cup cold water
4 eggs   2 cups confectionary sugar
¾ cup oil   juice of 2 lemons
1 pkg. yellow cake mix

                    --- Mix together and set aside-----

Combine jello, water and eggs--beat for 2 minutes. Add cake mix and oil and beat for 1 minute or until well incorporated.

Pour into a 9x12 greased pan' Bake @350 deg. For 40 minutes

Remove from oven and immediately prick the top of the entire cake with a fork. Pour the confectionary sugar and lemon juice mixture all over top.

Allow to set and cool before cutting.

Lemon Cheese Cake

Bottom layer---

2 cups vanilla wafer crumbs
Add ½ stick butter-melted   -----   mix together and place in bottom of
Pan and up on the edges.

Bake @325 deg. For 8-10 minutes

Beat---

3-8 oz. pkgs. of cream cheese
1 cup sour cream
1 cup sugar
2 eggs
1 tbsp. lemon juice
1 tbsp. lemon zest

Pour in pan and bake @ 325 deg. For 25 minutes.

** top with jam or lemon curd

Blueberry Cheese Cake

For the crust

2 pkgs. graham crackers
1 stick butter-melted

Place 5 whole crackers in a plastic bag and crush into fine crumbs.
Place crumbs in a bowl and mix thoroughly with melted butter.
Press into a 9x13 -ungreased pan , (all the way up the edges of the pan.)

Batter---

1 8 Oz. Pkg. cream cheese- softened
1 egg
1 can (14 oz) sweetened, condensed milk
3 tbsp. lemon juice
1 can (21 oz.) of blueberry pie filling

Beat cream cheese and condensed milk until smooth for 2-3 minutes.
Add lemon juice and egg and beat on high speed for 1 minute.

Pour batter over graham cracker crust. Drop the pie filling with a spoon
At evenly placed intervals.

Bake @ 300 deg. For about 55 minutes.
Cool completely before cutting.

Carrot Cake

1-½ cup corn oil   2-½ tsp. vanilla
2 cups sugar   ½ tsp. salt
3 eggs   2 cups shredded carrots
2 cups flour   1 cup nuts-finely chopped
2 tsp. cinnamon
½ can crushed pineapple
   (drained well)

Pre-heat oven @ 350 deg.--

Mix the oil, eggs and sugar together . Add remaining ingredients and
Mix well.
Pour into 9x13 baking dish.

  Bake for 1 hour-- cool before cutting.

**Serve with a cream cheese topping-

Bread Pudding

**use day old, crusty bread--

1 lg. box raisins (the amount is optional)
2 sticks butter-softened
1-½ cups sugar
3 cups heavy cream
6 eggs -beaten
2 tbsp. vanilla
2 tbsp. cinnamon

Cut bread into cubes-enough to fill the pan-
Place bread cubes in baking pan.

Blend butter and sugar with a fork. Add beaten eggs, vanilla, cinnamon,
cream and add raisins. Mix well.

Pour over bread covering completely and toss until all the bread is soaked.
Allow to sit for 1-2 hours.

Bake @ 350 deg. Till done.

Strawberry Afternoon Delight

3 cans frozen strawberries- drained
2 bananas- mashed
½ cup pecans--chopped
1 can crushed pineapples--drained
1 container sour cream
1 pkg. strawberry jello
1 cup water--hot

Strain strawberries and pineapples. Put in bowl with crushed bananas. Add one cup of hot water to jello. Mix well until completely dissolved. Add to fruit and mix. Add pecans and blend together. Add ½ of mixture to a sprayed pan. Set up in fridge for 3 hours.

Spread 1 cup sour cream gently over top ,and put remaining mixture as top layer.
Keep refrigerated!

** Serve with whipped cream

Deep -Dark- Chocolate Cookies

2 pkgs. -8 square each, semi-sweet baking chocolate
¾ cup brown sugar--packed firmly
2 eggs
1 tsp. vanilla
½ stick margarine (or butter)
½ cup flour
¼ tsp. baking powder
2 cups nuts--finely chopped (optional)

* coarsely chop 1 pkg. chocolate--set aside

Pre-heat oven @ 350 deg.

In microwave-melt the remaining 8 squares of chocolate. Stir till smooth.
Mix in butter, sugar, eggs and vanilla till completely incorporated.

Stir in flour and baking powder. Add in reserved chopped chocolate and
nuts.
Drop by scant ¼ cupfuls onto an ungreased cookie sheet

Bake about 12-14 minutes.
    Cool before removing from pan.

Paximadia -----Greek Walnut Cookie Slices

3-xtra lg. eggs
1 cup Mazola oil
1 cup sugar
3 cups flour
1-½ cups walnuts-chopped
1-½ tsp. baking powder
½ tsp. salt
1 tsp. vanilla

Beat eggs and sugar . Add oil and beat until thick. Sift flour, baking powder and salt.
Add flour by spoonfuls to eggs and oil mixture.
Then add nuts and vanilla. Cover and refrigerate a few hours or overnight.

Divide dough in 3or 4 parts depending on how big you want the pieces.
Make 3 or 4 strips and stretch them out on an ungreased cookie sheet.

Once evenly put on cookie sheet -press palm of hand lightly on each strip to make it smooth and even.

Before baking, mix a little sugar and cinnamon and lightly spread on top Of each one.

Bake @ 350 deg. For 20 minutes. Remove tray and cut into pieces-Diagonally. (Size is optional)
With a spatula, turn cookies over and again sprinkle with sugar and cinnamon mixture. Return to oven and bake about 6-8 minutes.

Remove tray from oven and turn pieces over again and bake 6 more minutes.
   Cool on rack.

** So worth it !

Banana Split Cake

2 cups graham cracker crumbs
2 sticks margarine
2 eggs
1 cup sugar
4-5 bananas -sliced
1 lg. can crushed pineapples--well drained
1 cup nuts-chopped
1 lg. container whipped cream
Cherries --for decoration

Melt 1 stick of butter and mix in with the cracker crumbs.
Press mixture firmly into 9x12 baking pan covering sides of pan.

Mix----
1 stick butter
2 eggs   ---------   Combine and beat for 15 minutes
1 cup sugar   at medium speed.

Pour mixture over crumbs. Put sliced bananas over top-then pineapples and nuts.

Top with whipped cream and decorate with cherries.

** Any berry can be used for decoration.
                              Store in fridge!

Apple Coffee Cake

¾ cup vegetable oil
1 cup sugar
2 eggs
2 cups flour
1 tsp. baking soda
Pinch of salt

1 tsp. cinnamon
3 cups apples- peeled and sliced
½ cup nuts- chopped
½ cup chocolate chips
2 tsp. vanilla

Pre-heat oven @ 325 deg.
Grease and flour 10 inch tube pan.

Mix together the oil, sugar and eggs in a lg. bowl.   Add the flour, baking
soda, salt ,cinnamon and vanilla and blend.

Mix in the apples, nuts and chocolate chips. Spread the batter evenly in the
pan.
Bake for 40 minutes or until done. Cool before cake from pan.

** Serves 10-12

Squash Pie

2 cups squash
2 cups milk
1 cup sugar
2 eggs
2 tsp. cinnamon
¼ tsp. cloves
¼ tsp. nutmeg
1 tbsp. flour
1 tsp. salt
1 tsp. vanilla
Pinch of ginger

Beat eggs and ¾ cups sugar . Mix well until all the sugar is blended in.
Mix ¼ cup sugar with remaining dry spices and add to egg mixture till well
incorporated. Add vanilla.

Add the squash and milk ,alternating them a little at a time. Beat
For a minute or so. Pour into uncooked pie shell.

Bake @ 425 deg. For 10 minutes- then reduce heat to 400 deg. For 50
minutes..

Mom's Early American Pear Pie

6 cups firm pears-sliced
¾ cup sugar
1 tsp. cinnamon or nutmeg.
ready made pie crust--for top layer
pastry lined pie pan-- can be store bought
2 tbsp. flour
1-½ tbsp. butter

Pre-heat oven @ 425 deg.

Pare and slice pears. Mix together sugar, spices, and flour.
Add to pears and mix lightly.

Pour into pastry lined 9 inch pie pan. Dot with butter. Cover with top crust
making small slits over top.

Seal and flute the edges.
Bake for 35-45 minutes.

** Serve cooled with a thick slice of cheese!

This is simple and excellent!!

Strawberry Jello Cheesecake

1 lg. container strawberries--sliced and divided
3 pkgs. strawberry jello--sugar free
1-12 oz. pkg. cottage cheese
2 prepared graham cracker pans

Dissolve 2 pkgs. jello in 1 cup boiling water. Add 1 cup cold water.

Put in blender-add cottage cheese and blend till smooth. Fill 2 pans.
Set up in refrigerator.
Arrange sliced strawberries on top.

Then dissolve 3rd pkg. of jello with1 cup boiling water and 1 cup cold water.
Pour over both pies equally. Set up in fridge.

Then add remainder of strawberries on top and fill center of pies with
whipped cream.

Pear or Apple Crumble

6-8 pears or apples--peeled and sliced
½ cup brown sugar
1 tbsp. vanilla
1 tsp. cinnamon
2 tbsp. flour

Mix all these ingredients together-- and place in a baking pan spreading out the apples evenly.
    Topping--

1 cup flour
1 cup brown sugar
1 stick butter

Mix by hand until it's nice and crumbly. Spread on top to cover the fruit.

Bake @ 350 deg. For ½ hour.

Live life fully while you're here. Experience everything.
Take care of yourself and your friends. Have fun, be crazy,
be weird. Go out and screw up! You're going to anyway,
So you might as well enjoy the process.
Take the opportunity to learn from your mistakes:
Find the cause of your problem and eliminate it.

Don't try to be perfect; just be an excellent example of
  being human.

                    Author   ___Anthony Robbins___

Too often we underestimate the power of touch, a smile,
a kind word, a listening ear, an honest compliment, or
the smallest act of caring, all of which have the potential
to turn a life around.
.

                    Author   __Leo Buscaglia____

PENNSYLVANIA VOICES BOOK VIII

THE ARTIST'S JOURNAL, ART FOR A CAUSE

MARYANN PASDA DIEDWARDO
WITH PATRICIA PASDA AND JOE DIEDWARDO

authorHOUSE®

AuthorHouse™
1663 Liberty Drive, Suite 200
Bloomington, IN 47403
www.authorhouse.com
Phone: 1-800-839-8640

First published by AuthorHouse 5/4/2009

ISBN: 978-1-4389-4256-8 (sc)

Library of Congress Control Number: 2009902977

Printed in the United States of America
Bloomington, Indiana

This book is printed on acid-free paper.

Dedicated to a late World War II veteran Joseph J. Pasda, graduate of The Pennsylvania State University in 1949, his wife J. D. Pasda, artist, and the natural world.

Introduction

Art Journal

Is defined as the creation of a small work that is make by hand or purchased to promote purpose of art as a means of change in society.

Our book demonstrates how three Pennsylvania artists' journaling projects can change the viewer and teach art journaling as a way of life.

PART I
WHAT IS AN ART JOURNAL?

Art Journal

An art journal is a record of art lessons, experiences, encounters with subject that inspire. The journal becomes the foundation of the artist's work

Art journal to create your recorded visions based on life drawing experiences. Use the blank pages to follow the samples and create your unique artist journal. Use pen and ink, pencil, marker, charcoal, conte, graphite, colored pencil, color stix, watercolor pencil, gouache, watercolor paint or a combination of materials.

The Purpose of Journaling

A journal is a way to keep a record. List honest reactions, and/or likes and dislikes about subjects, ideas which may be new to you; self discovery art journaling is also a part of learning to draw and paint. A private journal is an alternative to show reflective writing and creative patterns that can be in sentence, poetry, or song lyrics that the artist writes or even electronic in nature like a website or CD. Art study through journaling can also engage artists to write on issues. Keep comments positive, pithy, and focused. Journal entries often help writers create art papers. Relate art entries to current events or life events as well.

Dialectical Journal

Take notes and sketch during your art journaling excursion on one side of the paper and write reflections and connections on the other side of the paper. The "dialogue" takes place between the written words and sketches on two sides of the paper and serves as a way of capturing thinking in art and writing forms. The artist makes observations about the use of powerful or moving objects, techniques, and stylistic devices.

Life in Art

I encourage artists to journal about experiences and essentially use them to prepare and succeed in final art projects. The journal is the doorway; the project completion will take a form that is based upon the initial idea.

We observe. The artist is analytical, logical, sequential, organized, on track. We learn to respond to natural world happenings like the sighting of a humming bird or a particular cloud pattern through how we see and feel, not with statements of right and wrong. Respond to the natural world. Participate in life drawing art at least once per week or more. We are guided by meaningful tasks in life so we have a sense of purpose to help others.

Therefore, we can create art about topics through a life story perspective. Begin art journaling with your own story. Filter the story as a metaphor throughout the works. If artists write stories, select those that are vivid, and include them as journey ideas, they are finding their own visions to begin their own art paths and their own "journeys." In the journaling pages that follow, through art and writing, develop stories through graphic means with line, form, space, color and texture to ignite an inner journey toward a clear artistic style.

Use dramatic art techniques to write the life story, and you will see your art soar. Build a setting, a character, define prior circumstances, work from moment to moment, use sense memory, uncover circumstance surround an object, find the composition of the piece of art which is the same as a role or story or play.

Ultimately, art is a personal journey determined by the mind, spirit, emotional ability of the creator to try to find a vision and to understand personal style. Therefore, artists listen to their own visions first then place the images on the pages.

PART II
JOURNAL EXAMPLES

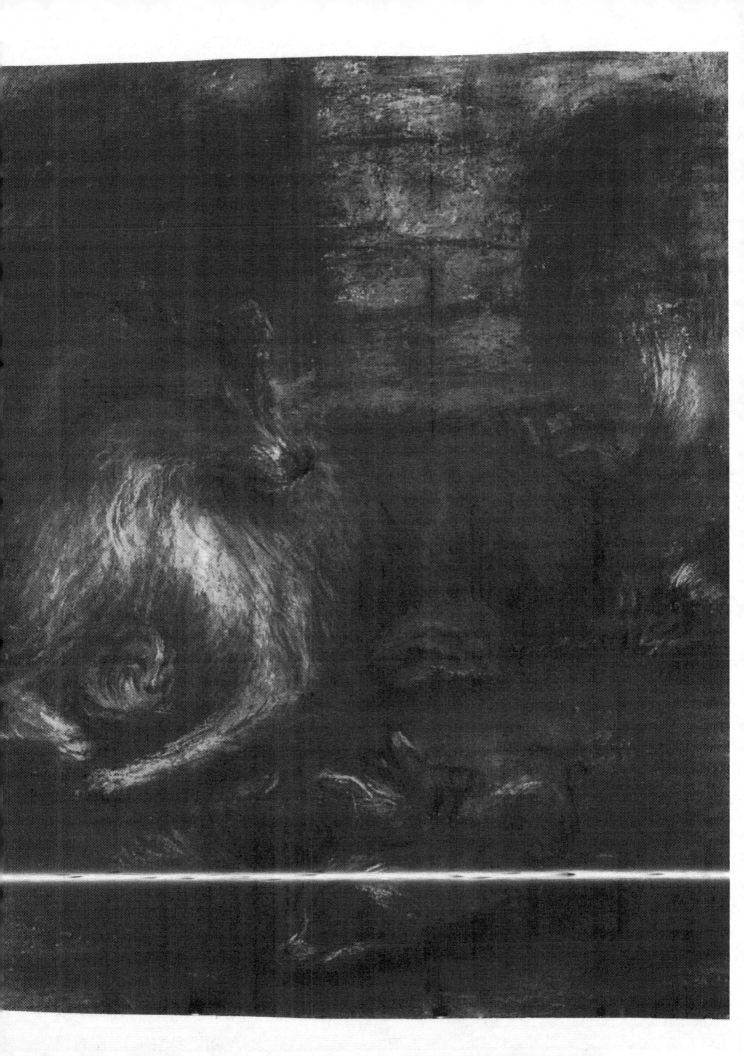

The Angel of the Tempest

Part III
Artist's Journal Pages

About the Artists

Maryann Pasda DiEdwardo, B.A., M.A., Ed.D. with her sister and co-author Patricia J. Pasda, B.F.A., M.F.A., her son and consultant, Joseph A. DiEdwardo, present a series of works that depict art as purpose for change.